Disinheriting
Uncle Sam

Disinheriting Uncle Sam

An Estate Planning Guide
for Illinois Residents

by

Laurence J. Kline, J.D.

Vireo
Publishing
Chicago, Illinois

Library of Congress Catalog Card Number: 99-93789

International Standard Book Number: 0-9671497-0-3

A Note to Readers

Most books dealing with estate planning are designed for a national audience. State laws, however, vary widely among the jurisdictions, and what may be the majority view may not be the law in the reader's state. While many of these books are very good, they must, inevitably, shortchange the reader because they are not specific enough.

This book is written especially for Illinois residents by an Illinois attorney. It offers the exact information an Illinois resident needs to effectively plan his or her estate. For example, it covers Illinois probate procedure, the Illinois law of intestate succession, and the Illinois estate tax. While much of estate planning involves the avoidance of the federal estate tax, it is very important to understand the Illinois rules governing estates and trusts in formulating any plan.

Non-Illinois residents should also find this book useful. The book usually indicates which position is the majority view and discusses areas where the states differ. Illinois tends to be in the mainstream with respect to most issues, so most of the Illinois laws discussed in this book will be similar to those in other states. The federal estate tax law and the methods of avoiding it are applicable in all states. Non-Illinois residents will learn what they need to deal effectively with their estate planning attorney, and can then rely on their attorney to explain the specific provisions of their local law.

I have tried to make this book useful by providing specific recommendations and advice wherever possible. However, everyone's situation is unique, and laws change, so please be aware that there is no substitute for using a qualified estate planning advisor to determine which planning techniques are appropriate for you and how they should be applied to your situation.

To Cindy

The author would like to acknowledge the assistance of the many persons who helped with this book: Ben Baldwin, Irv Blackman, Jim Cook, Paul Glick, Alec Harris, Brad Heywood, Sam Kruger, Jim Maivald, Jordan Miller, Gary Scholnick, Dale Taylor, Dick Zachar, and especially my family, Cindy, Jeff, and Jenny, for their encouragement and assistance. I am very grateful to Wendy Durkin for her careful review of the text and her helpful comments.

Table of Contents

Introduction

Untold millions of dollars in estate taxes are needlessly paid into the federal coffers each year, solely because people do not take the time to properly plan their estates. Even more frustrating are the wasted tax dollars expended by the estates of people who had the proper estate planning documents, but who did not thoroughly understand the way in which their assets should be titled in order to take advantage of the tax-saving techniques built into those documents.

As its title suggests, this book is filled with suggestions on how to disinherit your favorite uncle. However, I will cover more than tax avoidance—my goal is to present a comprehensive review of the entire estate planning process.

I have spent 27 years in the practice of law, concentrating exclusively in the areas of estate planning and the administration of estates and trusts. I have met with thousands of people to plan their estates and have attempted to teach them as much as possible about the estate planning process so that they could make intelligent decisions. However, there is never enough time during our meetings to fully impart to my clients all that they should know. Also, because many people learn better visually than aurally, there is a need to put into written form all of the information a person needs in order to work effectively with his or her estate planning attorney.

As noted, this is a book is about *estate planning*, which is the process of passing your accumulated wealth to your beneficiaries, either in trust or outright, either upon death or during lifetime, with a minimum of transfer taxes and administration expenses. Two topics that will be thoroughly covered will be *tax avoidance* and *probate avoidance*. There will also be several chapters dealing with the drafting of the estate plan, a subject often ignored in books of this type.

I will not offer advice about how to build up your estate—that is a job for your investment advisor. I will not provide extensive

guidance in avoiding income taxes—that is a job for your accountant. Nor will I offer recommendations as to how much and what
kind of insurance you should have—that is a job for your insurance
agent (though I will show you how to shelter your life insurance
from estate taxes). As you will soon see, there is more than enough
about the estate planning process to fill this book, even though it
covers only the basic estate planning techniques.

Here is a brief overview of the organization of this book:

- Chapters 1-3 provide basic background information on disposing of property, asset ownership, the probate process, and
  dealing with disability.

- Chapters 4-8 cover the four cornerstones of a basic estate plan
  —the living trust (and its funding), the pourover will, the
  power of attorney for property, and the advance health care
  directive.

- Chapter 9 is a basic primer on the transfer tax system, covering
  estate, inheritance, and gift taxes.

- Chapter 10 discusses the estate tax shelter trust—the primary
  estate tax savings tool for a married couple. Chapter 11 covers
  asset ownership for couples who use this trust, and Chapter 12
  examines its drafting.

- Chapters 13-16 complete the discussion of the drafting process,
  providing a useful preview of the concepts you will be discussing with the estate planning attorney, including trusts for
  children and the selection of executors, trustees, and guardians.
  In particular, Chapter 14 covers the concept of generation-
  skipping—an estate planning technique that has the potential of
  eventually saving millions of dollars in even relatively modest
  estates, but which is too little utilized by planners and their
  clients.

- Chapters 17-24 look at some additional estate planning concepts and techniques—gift giving, life insurance planning, retirement plan beneficiaries, charitable gifts, creditor protection, and Medicaid planning.

- Chapter 25 revisits a couple first introduced in Chapter 1 to show how the use of some of the techniques discussed in this book can significantly save on taxes and expenses, and greatly shorten and simplify the administrative process.

Throughout the text, important words and phrases applicable to the estate planning process will be highlighted in italics. All of these are defined in a glossary at the end. There are also a number of diagrams and tables that illustrate the estate planning techniques discussed in this book.

I hope you find this book helpful as you contemplate one of life's disagreeable but absolutely necessary endeavors—planning for your incapacity and demise.

Chapter 1
Henry and Helen

When her husband Henry died in 1999, Helen was very concerned about her financial situation. She had little idea of the extent of their assets, and she dreaded the process of dealing with her husband's estate. However, she soon learned from their long-time accountant that she and Henry owned $1,000,000 in assets and that she was the beneficiary of a $200,000 life insurance policy. The accountant explained that because all of their non-insurance assets were in joint tenancy, there would be no probate proceeding and she was now the sole owner of all of the couple's assets. The accountant also informed Helen there would need to be both a federal estate tax and a state estate tax return filed, but Helen was pleased to discover that there were no death taxes of any kind due on Henry's estate because of the unlimited marital deduction for death tax purposes. Helen was, to her great surprise, a millionaire.

Helen remembered that when their children, Tom and Sally, were young, she and Henry had signed wills providing that they would leave their estates to one another and, upon the death of the survivor, they would divide their combined estates equally between the children. She made a mental note to check with an attorney to see if this will was still appropriate. In the meantime, Helen decided that because joint tenancy had been so successful in avoiding probate at Henry's death, she would use the same method for her estate.

Helen was very careful to keep things equal between the two children. First, she made Tom the beneficiary of a new $100,000 life insurance policy she took out on her life, but at the same time made Sally the joint owner of a certificate of deposit in the same amount. Next, she made Sally the joint owner of the $300,000 brokerage account she had inherited from Henry and made Tom the joint owner of the house in which she lived, also worth $300,000. She retitled accounts at two other banks, totaling $400,000, into separate joint tenancy accounts with her children, $200,000 each. A third bank held the remaining $100,000, which she intended to split into two $50,000 accounts, one for each child. However, the bank was in another Chicago suburb 25 miles away, so she decided to take care of this the next time she was in that neighborhood.

Helen was very satisfied with her do-it-yourself estate plan. And, had she died immediately after establishing it, it would have worked quite well, leaving $650,000 to each child, although the $100,000 still in her name at the distant bank would have required a probate proceeding.

However, Helen didn't die right away—she lived for four more years. During this period of time the stock market was booming. Helen's brokerage account grew from $300,000 to $500,000. Because of this increase in her net worth, Helen no longer saw the need to pay the ever-increasing premiums on her term life insurance, so she dropped the policy. She remembered that the policy had been payable to one of the children, and realized that she would need to make an adjustment to her estate plan. She would take care of that as soon as she had some time.

Then Helen became ill. Sally, who lived nearby, took care of her as best she could. Tom, who lived on the east coast, could only visit occasionally. Eventually, Helen was no longer able to take care of herself. She and the children agreed that it was time she entered a nursing home. They found a lovely one nearby and, sadly, Helen moved out of her home of 40 years. Sally arranged with a real estate broker to list the home and it sold quickly, for an unexpectedly high price of $400,000.

Sally was glad that the house had sold rapidly so that her mother, who was not as mentally sharp as before, could still execute the necessary deeds. She learned from the real estate attorney that even though Tom was a joint tenant, if her mother had not been competent when the house was sold, the children would have been required to open a guardianship proceeding in probate court, obtain the court's approval of the sale, and thereafter account to the court annually as to the disposition of the proceeds.

Sally was still doing a lot for her mother. Among other responsibilities, she was managing Helen's finances. To facilitate this Helen agreed that the proceeds from the sale of the home should be deposited into a bank account on which Sally was a co-signer. Helen had a nagging remembrance that she had to keep things even, but her memory was not as good as it had once been. Besides, wasn't the joint tenancy arrangement the easiest way for Sally to handle her financial affairs?

Helen passed away in 2003. The children were surprised to learn that the $1,200,000 of assets that Helen had inherited from Henry were now worth $1,500,000. They—and particularly Tom— were even more surprised to discover that, of the $1,500,000, Sally was the surviving joint tenant as to $1,200,000, while Tom was the surviving joint tenant as to only $200,000, with $100,000 still in Helen's name. (Helen had never made that trip to the distant bank.)

Because the $100,000 account was in Helen's sole name, it was necessary to probate her estate. However, the old will that Helen had never gotten around to changing provided that all of the fees, expenses and estate taxes were to be paid out of the residue of her probate estate. The $100,000 in probate assets were woefully insufficient to pay the estate taxes of more than $300,000, much less the fees and expenses of administration. The shortfall had to be paid from other property. Because Helen died in Illinois, which does not have a statute determining the apportionment of taxes and expenses, the children soon began to argue about who was responsible for the balance of those charges.

Tom, of course, was not happy about the way in which the estate was divided. He believed that the terms of his mother's will should be carried out, regardless of the joint tenancy holdings. Sally, somewhat resentful of the fact that she had done so much for her mother and that Tom now wanted an equal share, consulted a lawyer. She learned that if she agreed to give some of the joint tenancy property to Tom, there might be some adverse gift tax consequences to herself. Meanwhile, Tom's lawyer told him that he might be able to recover part of the joint tenancy based on the doctrine of "joint tenancy for convenience only," but warned Tom that this might be difficult to prove.

Tom filed suit attempting to force Sally to turn over the joint tenancy property to the probate estate and to have the court determine the apportionment of the excess estate taxes. Sally, incensed that her brother had resorted to litigation, instructed her attorney to defend the case vigorously. Eventually, after considerable time and expense, cooler heads prevailed and a settlement was reached. The settlement agreement provided that after taxes, expenses, and fees, Sally inherited about $700,000 and Tom less than $400,000. More than $400,000 had disappeared in taxes, expenses, and attorneys' fees.

Is this a true story? No, not exactly. At least, it didn't all happen within one family. But I have seen every one of these facts occur in numerous situations, and so have most other experienced estate planners. It is illustrative of what happens when well-meaning people attempt to construct their own estate plans.

The fact that any estate taxes were payable is attributable to the couple's decision to leave all of their assets directly to one another. With only a negligible loss of control, and a minimum of administrative hassle, the couple could have saved all of the more than $300,000 paid in estate taxes by using the estate tax shelter trust technique explained in Chapter 10.

The need to probate the estate could have been avoided had Helen followed through with her intent to retitle the distant bank account in joint tenancy. It could also have been solved had Helen established a living trust and placed all of her assets in the trust, as discussed in Chapter 4.

The third major problem illustrated in this chapter—the inequality in distributions—could have been solved had Helen been scrupulously careful to keep things even between the children. However, I can tell you from experience that this type of planning almost never works. Helen made two mistakes: (1) she planned her distributions based on assets and dollars instead of percentages, and

(2) she failed to provide for the distribution of her entire estate pursuant to a single, comprehensive document—either a well-constructed will or a living trust.

The single-document/percentage-distribution approach to estate planning is a theme that will reappear in this book. For example, had Helen simply left all of her assets in her name, her old will would have properly disposed of her property. Even the tax apportionment issue would not have raised its ugly head, for Helen would have had sufficient probate assets for all taxes to be paid from her residuary probate estate, as her will directed. She could have had Sally manage her finances by executing a simple power of attorney for property.

Even better, Helen could have established a living trust to own all of her property. This technique would have provided Sally with the ability to manage Helen's affairs, would have avoided any probate proceedings, and would have properly disposed of all of Helen's assets at her death with almost no administrative costs.

We will revisit Henry and Helen in this book to illustrate some of the basic techniques presented. At the end, we will rewind and revise their lives a bit to illustrate how proper planning could have saved a great deal of money and grief.

Chapter 2
The Ownership of Property—Part One

The first step in the estate planning process is to understand how property can be owned and how its ownership affects the way in which it is transferred at death.

SOLE OWNERSHIP

For many people, property ownership is a simple decision. When they put money into a new bank account, buy a car or a home, or invest in stocks or bonds, they want the property titled in their own name. Such property is held in *sole ownership*.

Property held in sole ownership passes at death in accordance with the terms of a *will*, also known as a *last will and testament*. If there is no will, property in sole ownership passes in accordance with the *law of intestate succession*, which is more fully described in the next chapter.

JOINT OWNERSHIP

Many people—particularly married couples—prefer to hold their property in *joint ownership*. There are three basic types:

Joint Tenancy With Right of Survivorship

The most common form of joint ownership is *joint tenancy with right of survivorship*. Under this type of ownership the property passes automatically to the surviving joint tenant upon the death of either joint tenant. Joint tenancy with right of survivorship is often referred to as joint tenancy. In this book, *joint tenancy* will describe property held not only in joint tenancy with right of survivorship, but in tenancy by the entireties, discussed in the next paragraph.

Tenancy By the Entireties

Most states, including Illinois, have a form of ownership known as *tenancy by the entireties* that creates the same post-death result as joint tenancy with right of survivorship. In Illinois, tenancy by the entireties can be used only by spouses and only with respect to real property. It is preferable to joint tenancy with right of survivorship because the property held in this fashion is protected from the creditors of either spouse, although a creditor of both spouses may levy against the property. Married couples who own their residence in joint tenancy with right of survivorship should consider switching to tenancy by the entireties.

Tenancy in Common

A third form of joint ownership between two or more people is called *tenancy in common*. This form of ownership does not cause the property to pass to the other tenants at death. Each tenant, in effect, owns an equal share of the property as sole owner. This is the least desirable form of joint ownership and has limited use.

Community Property

There are nine states that have created another type of ownership for spouses known as *community property*. These states are Arizona, California, Idaho, Louisiana, Nevada, New Mexico, Texas, Washington, and Wisconsin.

In a community property state, a spouse's compensation earned during marriage, including the earnings and appreciation on that compensation, is community property in which each spouse is deemed to have an undivided one-half interest. Property acquired before the marriage, and gifts and inheritances received during the marriage, are separate property. Earnings on separate property during marriage can either be community or separate property, depending on the state. The way in which property is titled is irrelevant to the determination of whether or not it is community property.

Community property is not automatically inherited upon death. Each member of the couple may dispose of his or her half of the community property at death as desired.

Probate Property

Property held in sole ownership, including property held in tenancy in common, is *probate property*. This means that upon disability or death this type of property is subject to a probate proceeding. In addition, any property such as insurance and retirement accounts payable to the decedent's executor or estate will also be subject to probate.

Non-Probate Property

There are a variety of ways of owning property so that it avoids probate:

Joint Tenancy

Property held in joint tenancy with right of survivorship or in tenancy by the entireties is non-probate property, because it passes on death by operation of law to the surviving tenant (or tenants). There is one important exception to this rule. If the joint tenants die simultaneously, in most states the property is treated as if it were in tenancy in common, *i.e.*, it passes in equal shares through the probate estate of each separate tenant.

Property With a Beneficiary Designation

Certain types of property pass at death pursuant to a *beneficiary designation*. Two common examples of such property are life insurance and retirement accounts. Also, in many states, including Illinois, a person can title a bank account or other property with the designation "payable on death" or "in trust for." This designation will cause the property to pass at death to the named beneficiary. Such accounts are known as *Totten trusts*. Savings bonds and other Treasury securities can also have a payable on death designation.

Trusts

Property held in trust is also non-probate property. For example, when you place property in a trust for yourself, you cease to be the owner of the property, but become the *beneficiary*. The trustee (which can be you) owns the property. Your death does not affect the ownership of the property. The trust continues to own the property just as it did before your death. In almost all states— including Illinois—no judicial proceedings are required to transfer property held in trust on death. The only changes in the trust on your death are:

- If you were the trustee, a successor trustee must step in upon your death.

- The trust beneficiaries change from you to those persons whom you want to receive the property after your death.

The trust will be further defined and the most commonly used trust—the living trust—will be discussed in detail in Chapter 4.

Chapter 3
The Probate Process

If ever a word has achieved a universal negative connotation, it is the word *probate*. While probate is best avoided, the probate process is not as time-consuming and costly as many writers would have us believe. The following is, I believe, a fair evaluation of the probate process.

Post-Death Probate

The purpose of a post-death probate proceeding is to provide a judicial forum in which:

- the rights of the estate's beneficiaries are protected by the court;

- claims against the decedent's estate are barred if not timely filed; and

- the right to contest the decedent's will is barred if a will contest is not timely filed.

These are important protections for the estate and its beneficiaries, and they should not be totally ignored. In some situations I have probated an estate, even though a formal probate was not required, for the sole purpose of placing a deadline on claims or will contests.

Is Probate Time-Consuming?

Probate gets its reputation for being time-consuming because there is a perception that it takes years to "clear probate." Yet in most states the actual probate process lasts less than a year from start to finish. Why, then, is probate so widely-perceived as taking so much time?

Many estates that go through probate are required to file a federal and/or a state death tax return. The federal return is due nine months after date of death; the state return is usually due at that time (as is the case in Illinois) or from one to six months later. The audit process connected with these returns ranges from six months to several years, depending on the complexity of the estate. In many states, the probate estate cannot be closed in court until these tax proceedings have been completed. So, the last step in the administrative process is the closing of the probate estate, even though the reason for the delay in most cases is an estate tax audit completely unconnected with the probate proceeding. Because probate is the final step, it is often unfairly blamed for the delay.

Is Probate Costly?

Probate also has a reputation for being expensive, usually as to the fees charged by the estate's attorney. This stems from the days in which Illinois attorneys charged on the basis of a probate fee schedule (often adopted by the local bar association with the approval of the probate court) that charged a fee on the basis of a percentage of the probate estate, with no consideration of the time spent by the attorney. Because it often takes just as long to sort out the administrative details of a small estate as a large one, the fee schedule was designed to fairly compensate an attorney handling a smaller, but somewhat complex, estate. For larger or simpler estates, the lawyer received a windfall.

The U. S. Supreme Court has determined that using a fee schedule established by the local bar constitutes an improper method of charging fees. This does not mean that an individual attorney cannot set his or her fee as a percentage of the estate. However, such a fee must appropriately compensate the attorney for time, expertise, and risk.

Most Illinois attorneys no longer charge a percentage of the estate, but instead charge based on time spent, or may charge a pre-agreed fixed fee designed to take into account all relevant factors with respect to the estate being probated. The result is lower attorney's fees for probating estates in Illinois. (Some other states have statutory fee schedules that can sometimes result in high fees.)

Should Probate Be Avoided?

Having pointed out some advantages of a post-death probate proceeding, and having minimized the disadvantages usually ascribed to it, it is nevertheless appropriate to ask: should probate be avoided? In general, the answer is yes. Most estates do not have significant claims nor anyone who wants to contest the decedent's dispositive plan. In most situations, the beneficiaries will be appropriately protected by the decedent's chosen personal representative and, if that representative does not properly carry out his or her duties, there is judicial redress available.

Even though post-death probate does not last as long and is not as expensive as most people fear, what delay and extra expense is present can be easily avoided through the establishment of a living trust. The added ability of the living trust to avoid pre-death probate proceedings in the event of incompetency clearly tilts the scale toward using this probate avoidance technique, which is discussed in Chapter 4.

Small Estate Affidavit

Most states have a procedure that allows a small estate to avoid post-death probate. In Illinois such a procedure is available for estates with no real estate holdings and with probate assets of less than $50,000. Any interested party may complete a *small estate affidavit* and send it to the institutions or persons holding the decedent's probate property, who are then required to turn the assets over to that party. In the affidavit, the interested party must swear that the assets will be used to pay all debts of the decedent and that any excess funds will be distributed in accordance with the decedent's will or, if there is no will, in accordance with the laws of intestate succession. Some states require that a certain number of days have passed from the decedent's death before a small estate affidavit can be used; Illinois does not.

Intestacy

No discussion of post-death probate procedures would be complete without touching on what happens when a person dies without a will. When this happens, the decedent is said to be *intestate*. An intestate estate goes through a probate proceeding just like a testate estate, but with these important differences:

- A judge determines who will be the personal representative in charge of administering the estate. Though most states, such as Illinois, designate who has the preference to nominate or act as the personal representative (depending on the degree of relationship to the decedent), the court makes the ultimate decision as to who will be named.

- In most states, including Illinois, unless the decedent has waived surety on the personal representative's bond in his or her will, the estate must pay an insurance company to post a surety bond on behalf of the estate. This fee usually runs between 1% and 2% of the value of the estate.

- Because the decedent did not leave instructions as to how the probate property should be distributed, in all states the estate assets will pass in accordance with the *law of intestate succession* as determined by the state legislature. The Illinois law of intestate succession is summarized in the box on the next page.

The Illinois Law of Intestate Succession

If there is a surviving spouse and no descendants, all to the spouse.

If there is a surviving spouse and descendants, one half to the spouse and one half to the descendants.

If there is no surviving spouse, but there are descendants, all to the descendants.

If there is no surviving spouse and no descendants, the property passes in equal shares to the decedent's parents and siblings, with a sole surviving parent taking a double share, and the descendants of a deceased sibling taking their parent's share.

If there is no spouse, descendants, parents, siblings, or descendants of siblings, the law provides for distribution to the closest ancestor either living or to the then living descendants of the decedent's closest ancestor who has then living descendants.

If there are no identifiable relatives, the estate *escheats* either to the county or the state (though it can be recovered if relatives are ever found).

There is no distinction between relatives of the whole and the half blood.

Any share passing to descendants of a person is distributed in equal shares to the person's surviving children, with the share of any child who predeceased the decedent, but who has then living descendants, passing to those descendants.

- There are many questions that can arise during the administration of an estate for which statutory or case law provide no clear-cut answers. The apportionment of taxes and expenses is one example, as pointed out in Chapter 1. Good estate planning attorneys routinely deal with such questions in the boilerplate provisions of their estate planning documents. However, a person dying without a will provides no guidance with respect to these matters—leaving the estate vulnerable to costly disputes to be resolved by the courts.

Pre-Death Probate (Guardianship)

Incompetency—any mental or physical incapacity that renders a person unable to manage his or her financial affairs—deserves as much consideration in the planning process as death. As in the case of post-death probate, the statutory system designed to deal with incompetency involves a proceeding in the probate court.

The probate court is authorized to verify incompetency, appoint a guardian, and supervise the handling of the incompetent's financial affairs. The guardianship proceeding requires someone—usually a relative—to petition the court to confirm the incompetence of the person. The court will normally rely upon the report of a physician to help it determine incompetency. However, if there is any question as to whether or not the person is incompetent, the court will require that the alleged incompetent be brought to court for questioning by the judge, a proceeding that is often demeaning and emotionally-draining for the family.

An attorney will normally have to be hired to assist the family through the incompetency proceeding. Once appointed, the guardian must post a surety bond at a significant annual cost to the incompetent's estate, and must provide to the court a detailed annual accounting of all receipts and disbursements. Moreover, any expenditures from the incompetent's estate must be pre-approved by the court, which can be a costly process in both time and money.

Illinois has recently joined a growing number of states that have passed what are known as *substituted judgment laws*. Such laws

grant to a guardian of the estate a number of powers not tradition-
ally held by such a guardian, so long as they are exercised by order
of court and with notice to all interested parties. In Illinois, these
include the power to:

- make gifts;
- create or amend trusts;
- modify an existing will;
- change beneficiary designations;
- execute disclaimers; and
- exercise powers of appointment.

These powers can be useful if it is necessary to implement
changes to an incompetent person's estate plan. However, they
should not be viewed as an excuse to postpone planning your estate.
The need to use the court system and the notice provisions required
to exercise these powers are guaranteed to create an expensive—and
perhaps litigious—situation. A little planning can completely avoid
the need for a probate incompetency proceeding. This is accomplished by a combination of a durable power of attorney for
property, an advance health care directive, and, ideally, a living
trust, all of which are covered in the next five chapters.

Chapter 4
The Living Trust

The living trust is regularly the subject of books and articles that tout it as superior to a will as the primary estate planning document. It is true that the living trust is an extremely effective estate planning tool and should be used by most people. However, it is not a panacea—people should understand the advantages and disadvantages of the technique before deciding whether or not they want to use a living trust as their primary estate planning instrument.

What is a Trust?

Trusts originated in feudal Britain when the lord went off to the crusades, enlisting a trusted friend, relative, or retainer to look after his properties. While simple in concept, the trust can sometimes be difficult to explain. For our purposes, a trust will be defined as follows:

- A trust is established by a written instrument, called a trust agreement.

- The trust agreement names a trustee, and should either identify one or more successor trustees or contain some mechanism for appointing successor trustees.

- The trust consists of property that is titled in the name of the trust or that becomes payable to the trust upon a contingency, such as life insurance proceeds on the death of an insured.

- The trust agreement instructs the trustee as to how to administer and distribute the trust property for the benefit of the beneficiaries during the trust term and upon the trust's termination.

That is a trust in a nutshell: a written agreement, a trustee, trust property, and instructions as to the administration and ultimate distribution of that property.

What is a Living Trust?

A living trust is a trust created during a person's lifetime into which the person places some or all of his or her assets. The living trust is almost always revocable, meaning that it can be modified or terminated by its creator. The person who creates the trust—the *grantor* or *settlor*—usually names himself or herself as the initial trustee, in which case the trust is sometimes referred to as a *self-declaration of trust*.

The primary advantage of the living trust is that it avoids probate proceedings if the grantor places his or her assets into the trust during lifetime. Because these assets are owned by a trust, they are not subject to the jurisdiction of the probate court. The living trust avoids the post-death probate process by directing the trustee —upon the grantor's death—either to hold the property in trust for designated individuals and/or to make distributions of the trust property to named beneficiaries.

The trust agreement, therefore, becomes a substitute for a will. Nevertheless, it is important that a *pourover will* also be executed, which provides that any assets not transferred into the trust during lifetime are "poured over" to the trust following the grantor's death.

If there are no probate assets, the will is simply filed, but not probated. The pourover will is discussed in greater detail in Chapter 6.

Other Advantages

In addition to probate avoidance, the living trust has several other advantages:

Privacy

The living trust offers privacy as to the disposition of a decedent's estate. Unlike a will, a living trust is not filed with the court and does not become a matter of public record.

Ease of Execution

A living trust does not require the formalities of execution that a will does. In many states, including Illinois, it is sufficient for the grantor to simply sign his or her name as grantor and as trustee, without witnesses.

Avoidance of Incompetency Proceedings

Although in theory a power of attorney for property avoids the need for an incompetency proceeding, powers of attorney are not always honored unless they specifically refer to the asset in question. As a result, I have learned over the years that the best way to avoid probate is with a fully-funded living trust.

Reduced Administration Fees

Because a living trust avoids probate, its use almost always results in lower post-death administrative fees. However, as discussed in Chapter 3, many states have now streamlined their probate procedures so that they are not nearly as expensive as they once were. The most time-consuming activities are the collection of assets, payment of expenses, compliance with tax proceedings, investment of assets, and distribution of the property, which occur whether or not there is a probate proceeding.

Possible Avoidance of Claims and Contests

Because the decedent's heirs and creditors are not required to receive notice when a trust is used, as they are in the probate process, it is probable that there will be fewer claims and disputes with respect to a trust than in a probate situation.

Disinheritance of Spouse

A little known "advantage" of the living trust is that in some states, including Illinois, it can provide a legitimate mechanism for circumventing the surviving spouse's *statutory share* of the deceased spouse's estate. In Illinois, the statutory share is the right given to a surviving spouse by statute to receive either one third (if there are children) or one half (if there are no children) of the deceased spouse's estate despite receiving a smaller bequest (or no bequest) in the decedent's will.

Funding the Living Trust

To be fully effective as a probate avoidance device, a person's assets must be funded into his or her living trust during lifetime. To do this, all real estate, bank accounts, stocks, bonds, partnership interests, insurance, retirement plans, IRAs, and other assets need to be reregistered or have their beneficiary designations changed. This process can be bothersome and time-consuming. Despite the best of intentions, some people do not complete this task, thus requiring a probate proceeding in addition to the administration of those assets that were placed into the trust. The trust funding process is covered in detail in the following chapter.

Misconceptions About Trusts

I have found over the years that many of my clients have misconceptions about trusts that, because of my familiarity with them, I sometimes fail to anticipate. You should be aware that:

- A trust is not supervised by any court or state agency. The court only takes action if a party to the trust requests it.

- A trust does not have to be located at or administered by a bank. Banks do frequently act as trustee, but it is not required. Most trusts have an individual as trustee.

- The trust assets do not have to be maintained at any one place. A trust consists of a collection of assets that you are free to have at a variety of different places, just as your own assets are. A trust might consist of a checking account at a bank, a certificate of deposit at a savings & loan, a brokerage account, some stock certificates in a safe deposit box, a partnership interest, and a condominium in Colorado. The common denominator is that all of these assets are registered in the name of the trust.

- A trust can be created by a trust agreement or in a will.

- Many trusts can be created in a single instrument. For example, a living trust often splits at death into a marital trust and an estate tax shelter trust. Upon the death of the surviving spouse, these trusts can be split into separate trusts for descendants.

Recommendations

I cannot say that a living trust is always better than using just a will, but it usually is:

- I strongly recommend the use of a living trust for older persons, typically those who have passed retirement age. Such people are more likely to benefit from a primary advantage of the living trust, which is the avoidance of a lifetime guardianship proceeding. Also, such people generally have more settled financial affairs, making it easier to reregister the person's assets into the trust. For the older unmarried person with any substantial amount of property, the living trust is, without question, the preferred estate planning technique.

- If I am planning a couple's estate, and have recommended that they divide their assets for tax-planning purposes as discussed in Chapter 11, I believe it makes sense to accomplish this and fund the trusts at the same time.

- For many other people, I usually recommend the use of an unfunded living trust to act as a recipient for insurance and, possibly, retirement plan proceeds. The trust can be funded either after execution or at any later time—the sooner the better. Post-death probate will be avoided so long as the living trust is funded before death.

- For a very few, I may recommend the use of a will as being the simplest way to provide for the post-death disposition of their property. When this is a couple, who probably hold most or all of their assets in joint tenancy, I usually recommend that as soon as one member of the couple dies, the survivor should definitely consider using the living trust.

Chapter 5
Funding the Living Trust

Merely executing a living trust is not enough to avoid probate—the trust must be *funded*. This is the process of reregistering or retitling assets into the name of the trust, or causing the trust to become the designated beneficiary of insurance, retirements plans, or other assets permitting a beneficiary designation. For those who will eventually create a living trust, this chapter is an important source of information to which you will want to refer. For all readers, this chapter may tell you whether or not the process of funding the trust is worth the effort.

Life Insurance

In keeping with my belief that—if possible—a single document should be used to dispose of the entire estate, life insurance should be made payable to the insured's trust as the primary beneficiary (unless ownership is transferred in order to save estate taxes as discussed in Chapters 19 and 20). The language that I recommend you use is, for example: "The acting trustee of the Henry A. Doe Trust dated December 19, 1998." The phrase "acting trustee" is used because it cannot now be determined exactly who the trustee will be at the time of the insured's death.

Some insurance companies insist on having the name of the trustee in the beneficiary designation. I have always thought this silly, for the present trustee is usually the insured, and it makes no sense to name the insured as beneficiary of his or her own insurance, even in the role of trustee. You could instead name the first successor trustee, but that person's eventual assumption of the role of trustee is subject to a number of contingencies. If the company insists on the name of the trustee, use the current trustee, even if it is the insured, unless they specify the use of the successor trustee.

Once your insurance is made payable to your trust, it should not be necessary to change the beneficiary again. The trust agreement can be amended as often as desired, and the beneficiary designation will remain the same.

Retirement Plans

Until you get to the detailed discussion on retirement plans in Chapter 21, you should be aware that many married people will want to designate the beneficiaries of their qualified retirement plans or IRAs as follows:

Primary beneficiary: The surviving spouse.

Secondary beneficiary: The acting trustee of the [name of decedent's trust] dated [date of trust].

Unmarried individuals will designate beneficiaries as follows:

Primary beneficiary: The acting trustee of the [name of decedent's trust] dated [date of trust].

Secondary beneficiary: None needed.

For example, Janet Smith, married to Jim Smith, would fill out the beneficiary designation form for her IRA as follows:

Primary beneficiary: My husband, James B. Smith

Secondary beneficiary: The acting trustee of the Janet L. Smith Trust dated April 22, 1990.

I caution you, however, that there are many exceptions to this general rule, and it is extremely important to study Chapter 21 and/ or work closely with your estate planning advisor in structuring the beneficiary designation for a retirement plan.

Other Assets

For most other assets, the person creating the living trust will want to transfer ownership to the living trust. The correct way to do this is to register such assets in the name of the trust, for example: "Henry A. Doe, as trustee of the Henry A. Doe Trust dated December 19, 1998." Exactly how this reregistration is accomplished will vary widely depending on the type of asset and the financial institution involved.

In general, each financial institution should be contacted and asked to provide the requirements for transferring an asset into a living trust. Most will ask you to complete a form and/or a signature card that they will provide. Some will simply ask you to write them a letter. Because each financial institution will have somewhat different requirements, it is impossible to provide a specific strategy that will work with every one. However, the following is a general guide to the transfer of the most common types of property:

Bank Accounts

The transfer of a bank account is usually accomplished by a signature card provided by your bank. If you retitle your checking account into the name of the trust, you should insist that the bank continue to show only your name on the face of the check, with no mention of the trust. People to whom you give checks may not understand, or may misinterpret, the reason you have a trust, and checks that disclose the trust relationship may not be as readily accepted.

Securities and Mutual Funds

If you hold securities in certificate form, this may be a good opportunity for you to go "paperless" by placing your assets into an account registered in the name of your trust. Such accounts can be established as a custody account at a bank, for which a small annual fee will be charged, or as a brokerage account at a securities firm, for which there is generally no charge (but as to which you may receive periodic calls from the broker with recommendations for purchases and sales). If you already have a securities account, you should obtain from the custodian or broker the necessary forms to reregister the account into the name of the trust.

If you opt to retain your certificates, they will need to be individually reregistered into the name of the trust. Generally, this is accomplished by completing (1) an *assignment separate from certificate*, also known as a *stock power* or *bond power*, and (2) an *affidavit of domicile*. These forms should be mailed to the transfer agent separately from the stock certificates, which should be sent by registered mail. You should contact each company's transfer agent to be certain you understand its specific requirements. If you don't want to do this yourself, many banks and brokerage houses will reregister your securities for a fee.

For securities firms, transfer agents, and mutual funds you will almost always be asked to provide a *medallion signature guarantee*, which can be obtained through financial services companies such as stockbrokers, banks, credit unions, and savings institutions that participate in the medallion signature guarantee program. No publicly-traded stock can be transferred without this type of guarantee. A notarized signature will not satisfy this requirement.

Many financial institutions will ask you to provide a copy of the entire trust agreement. This is not necessary. All the institution really needs is a copy of the first page, the section dealing with the trustee's powers, the section dealing with the appointment of successor trustees, and the signature page. I have on numerous occasions sent only these pages in response to a request for the entire document and have never been asked to supply more.

Due to the increase in the use of living trusts, many institutions now have a form on which you can certify the existence, date, trustee, and certain provisions of the living trust, in lieu of providing a copy of the trust agreement. This is a very sensible solution, one which permits you to retain the privacy of your dispositive provisions while saving the institution from having to store numerous documents.

Real Estate

Real estate is conveyed into a living trust by a *deed in trust*. I recommend that this deed be in the form of a warranty rather than a quitclaim deed, for this will extend the protection of your existing title insurance to the trust. Where title is currently either in joint tenancy with right of survivorship, tenancy by the entireties, or tenancy in common between spouses, I recommend that the property is first deeded to the spouse in whose trust the property is to be owned, and then deeded from that spouse into the trust. This prevents any argument that the spouse deeding away the property retains any interest in the other spouse's trust that would be taxable on the transferor's death for estate tax purposes.

Even though most of the transfers discussed in this chapter do not require the assistance of legal counsel, the deed or deeds discussed in the previous paragraph should be prepared by your attorney. Where out-of-state property is involved, your attorney may want to work with counsel in that state unless he or she is thoroughly familiar with the rules regarding real estate transfers in the other state. It is especially important to transfer out-of-state real property to the living trust in order to avoid *ancillary probate* (a probate proceeding in other than the decedent's home state) which can be both difficult and expensive.

Land Title Trusts

Illinois is one of only a few states to utilize a specialized form of trust know as a *land title trust*, which is used to own real property. The land trust, as it is usually called, allows property to be owned anonymously and can simplify the mortgage process. The trustee—usually a corporate trustee—holds legal title to the property; the owner of the property holds the *beneficial interest*. The land title trust document permits the holder of the beneficial interest to designate a successor holder of this interest upon death. Thus, a land title trust is a method of probate avoidance.

In keeping with my belief that a person's estate should be disposed of by a single document, I recommend that existing land trusts be amended to provide that the successor holder of the beneficial interest is the current holder's living trust, using the same language as with insurance, *e.g.*, "the acting trustee of the Henry A. Doe Trust dated December 19, 1998."

Tangible Personal Property

As part of the estate planning process I usually prepare a blanket assignment of *tangible personal property* (*i.e.*, property such as clothing, jewelry, furniture, and the like) to the trust. I usually provide in my trust agreements that the grantor can amend the provision disposing of the tangible personal property by a written memorandum lodged with the trust records, thus greatly simplifying the amendment process.

Certain types of tangible personal property, such as automobiles, boats, trailers, and so forth, are registered with the state. A blanket assignment of tangible personal property does not cause these items to become owned by the trust—it is necessary to retitle this type of property through the appropriate state agency. Many people in Illinois choose not to do so, instead relying on the Illinois Small Estate Affidavit that permits probate estates not exceeding $50,000 in value to effectively avoid probate. However, where these items, together with other probate assets, are likely to exceed $50,000, it is recommended that they be retitled in the name of the trust.

Partnership Interests

Where an interest is held in a partnership, it is often sufficient to write a letter to the general partner directing that the partnership interest be transferred to the trust. Sometimes, I have found the following simple assignment form to be useful with respect to assets such as these:

> I, Henry A. Doe, hereby assign, transfer, and convey all of my interest in the ABC Partnership to Henry A. Doe, as trustee of the Henry A. Doe Trust, dated December 19, 1998.

> _____
>   Henry A. Doe

The exact requirements will vary widely from partnership to partnership. It is also a good idea to have your attorney review the partnership agreement.

Summary

Funding a trust to avoid probate can be a lengthy process. However, financial institutions are finally catching on to the process, making it a bit more streamlined. I believe the probate avoidance achieved by a funded trust is well worth the time and effort. Also, the entire process of identifying and consolidating your assets makes it much easier for your chosen personal representative to handle your financial affairs upon incompetency or death.

I have handled situations where, upon the death of a single parent with assets less than the amount requiring a federal estate tax return, the trust has been fully administered and distributed within two or three months, enough time to make sure that all of the decedent's outstanding bills have been received and paid.

Chapter 6
The Pourover Will

Even though a living trust is used, the preparation and execution of a will is still an essential part of an estate plan. A will used in conjunction with a living trust is known as a *pourover will*, for its purpose is to take whatever probate assets may exist at the time of death and pour them over into the living trust. The will is also the document that must be used to appoint guardians for minor children, as will be discussed in more detail in Chapter 16.

Once signed, a pourover will rarely needs to be changed, unless the testator changes the executors or the guardians for minor children. Although the will needs to be filed with the probate court at death, it provides no information as to the ultimate disposition of the property, thus preserving the family's privacy.

If there are no probate assets at death, the filing of the pourover will is the only step that needs to be taken—there are no probate proceedings required. Even if there are some probate assets, almost all states permit the utilization of a small estate affidavit, or similar procedure, to avoid probate for small estates, as discussed in Chapter 3.

As discussed in more detail in Chapter 16, I recommend that the executor named in the will be the same person or corporation named as the successor trustee in the living trust. This simplifies the administration of the decedent's affairs if a probate administration or the use of a small estate affidavit is required.

Of course, a will can be used as the primary dispositive document. As previously noted, all of the tax savings methods available by using a living trust can also be achieved in a properly drafted will. For an estate with minimal probate assets and no living trust, a simple will is used to dispose of that property at death, utilizing a small estate affidavit as the method of administration.

Burial Instructions and Organ Donation

Many people are under the mistaken belief that a will is the appropriate place to provide for burial instructions or the donation of organs, tissue, or bodily remains. A will is only a legally effective document once it has been admitted by the probate court, a process that is measured in weeks, not days or hours. By the time the will is admitted, it is of no use in authorizing such donations.

Burial instructions, including directions as to cremation, are best handled in a separate letter of which your spouse and/or other family members have copies or know its location. A copy can also be lodged in advance with the funeral home of your choice.

Illinois residents who wish to record their wish to donate bodily organs or tissue should sign the back of their driver's licenses (or state ID cards). This can be done even after the license has been laminated by using a ball point pen (and writing very small). The signature needs to be witnessed by two adults. In addition, such individuals should join the Organ/Tissue Donor Registry maintained by the Illinois Secretary of State. This can be done at any Driver Services Facility or by calling 800-210-2106. Most other states have similar programs.

Those wishing to donate their remains for medical research and dissection should contact the Anatomical Gift Association of Illinois, a non-profit consortium of the eight medical schools in the state. The association will provide a form to be signed and lodged with them and a wallet card to be retained by the donor. The association can be contacted at 800-734-5283. Once the remains are no longer needed, they are cremated. The ashes can be returned to the family, if advance arrangements are made.

Burial, cremation, and organ donor instructions can also be placed in the power of attorney for health care, as discussed in Chapter 8.

Chapter 7
The Power of Attorney for Property

As discussed in Chapter 4, one of the reasons to use a living trust is to provide for the administration of a person's finances in the event of disability. While the living trust is the best method of dealing with this situation, it is not enough. An essential ingredient of a complete estate plan is a *power of attorney for property* by which an *agent* is appointed to deal with a person's assets in the event of disability. The person who creates a power of attorney is called a *principal*. I will use the terms agent and principal here and in the following chapter.

Why should there be a power of attorney for property even though there is a living trust? First, the trust may not be fully funded when the principal becomes incompetent. If there is no agent appointed, the only way to deal with the principal's probate assets (*i.e.*, assets titled in the principal's name) is to appoint a guardian in a probate proceeding. A power of attorney for property can empower the agent to transfer assets into the trust, thus ensuring that the estate plan works smoothly and effectively.

Also, even if the trust has been fully funded, there will usually be transactions that the trustee is not permitted to handle, such as:

- dealing with transactions involving joint tenancy assets where both joint tenants are required to sign, such as the sale of real estate,

- handling an audit of the principal's personal income tax return,

- dealing with the principal's retirement plans, and

- interacting with government agencies such as Social Security, Medicare, and the Veterans Administration.

I can tell you from experience that a comprehensive power of attorney for property is an invaluable tool in avoiding lifetime probate proceedings, even where a living trust has been incorporated into the estate plan.

Durable Power

Formerly, the law of most states was that a power of attorney became void upon the disability of the principal, under the belief that the law should prevent an agent from doing that which could not be done by the principal. Unfortunately, this prevented the use of a power of attorney in exactly those circumstances where it was most needed. With this law in effect, a disabled person's family was forced to go to probate court for the appointment of a guardian or conservator.

Within the past few decades, virtually all states, including Illinois, have adopted laws that permit a power of attorney to remain in effect even after the principal becomes disabled. Such a power is called a *durable power of attorney*. The statutory power of attorney for property discussed in this chapter is a durable power.

Statutory Forms

Most states have adopted what are referred to as *statutory powers of attorney*—standard forms approved by the legislature for use by its citizens and others wishing to utilize a form of power of attorney readily acceptable within that state. The statutory forms often provide for boxes to be checked or initialed, blanks to be filled in, or sections to be crossed-out, but otherwise require that the entire statutory form be used. Statutory forms are much more readily accepted by financial institutions than custom-drafted forms, as the institution does not need to have its legal department analyze the document to determine if the agent has the necessary authority to act on the principal's behalf.

I wholeheartedly endorse the use of statutory forms and use them regularly in my practice. It is possible to add, subtract, or modify powers within the standard form so that they can accomplish any desired purpose. The statutory forms are not the only forms permitted; if necessary, a separate power of attorney can be drafted. For example, the Illinois statutory form does not permit more than one agent to act at a time, so I will draft a custom power of attorney when a client feels it is necessary to have co-agents.

Even though statutory forms are available in pre-printed form at stationery stores, most of my clients prefer that I prepare the form so that I can interpret it for them, assist them in making any desired modifications, and supervise its execution. One power I always add is the power of the agent to transfer the principal's assets to the principal's living trust. In this way, the agent can essentially terminate his or her responsibility over the principal's property by transferring any probate assets into the living trust where they can be effectively administered by the successor trustee. Another frequently-added and useful power is the power to continue gift programs instituted by the principal.

Selection of Agents and Successors

One of the most important decisions you will make in completing a power of attorney for property is the identity of your agent and successor agents. Generally, you will want to name as agent the same person who will be acting as your executor and trustee, and the successor agents should match up with the successor executors and trustees. The exception is when you have appointed a bank or trust company as successor trustee, for most corporate fiduciaries will not act under a power of attorney. As with executors and trustees, I recommend that husbands and wives designate identical successor agents.

The Illinois statutory power of attorney for property provides that—unless the principal provides otherwise—the agent is automatically nominated as guardian of the estate, if one is required. Although an agent can be granted extensive powers, there are certain very useful powers set forth in Chapter 3 with regard to the modification of a person's estate plan that only a guardian of the estate can exercise.

Chapter 8
Advance Health Care Directives

While they are not documents that deal with the administration and disposition of property, advance health care directives have been an important part of my practice for many years. I consider pre-planning for an incapacitating or terminal illness an essential aspect of the estate planning process. There are two documents that need to be explained in connection with health care planning.

Living Will

The most widely known advance health care directive is the *living will*, not to be confused with the living trust. A living will is a general expression of a person's intent that no heroic or extraordinary measures are to be taken in the event of a terminal illness. The living will has been adopted in statutory form by 47 states and the District of Columbia. Only Massachusetts, Minnesota, and New York have not done so. The Illinois form of living will is set forth at the end of this chapter.

Power of Attorney for Health Care

I rarely use living wills in my practice, for there is a better document available in Illinois—the *power of attorney for health care*. A document of this type is available in every jurisdiction except Alaska, although it may have a different name (such as the *health care surrogate form* or *advance medical directive*). The power of attorney for health care differs from the living will in that it appoints an agent (or surrogate) to make health care decisions if you are incapacitated. The advantage, of course, is that in the event of an intra-family disagreement, the appointed agent has the authority to resolve the situation without court intervention.

As mentioned in connection with the power of attorney for property, the appointment of successor agents under a health care power is of particular importance, especially for a married couple who have presumably named one another as primary agents. I often find that husbands and wives select different successor agents in their health care powers, particularly if the children are too young or otherwise unsuitable to handle this role. A medical professional can be named as agent under your power of attorney for health care so long as he or she does not provide health care services to you.

Another advantage of the health care power of attorney versus the living will is the ability to customize the language giving guidance to the health care agent. The Illinois form, for example, contains three optional paragraphs that provide guidance to the agent as to the use of life-sustaining treatment. Nearly all of my clients choose to initial the following paragraph:

> I do not want my life to be prolonged nor do I want life-sustaining treatment to be provided or continued if my agent believes the burdens of the treatment outweigh the expected benefits. I want my agent to consider the relief of suffering, the expense involved, and the quality as well as the possible extension of my life in making decisions concerning life-sustaining treatment.

The Illinois form also permits language to be added that sets forth any personal directives with respect to your health care. In this section, many of my clients address such issues as artificial nutrition and hydration, respiratory ventilation, and cardiac resuscitation.

The power of attorney for health care also allows you to direct your agent regarding burial, cremation, and the donation of organs, tissue, and bodily remains. Normally an agent's authority ceases at death, but for purposes of carrying out these directives, an agent's authority continues for a reasonable period.

A final advantage of the health care power of attorney is that it deals not only with a terminal illness, but with any situation where you are unable to make your own decision about your health care, such as unconsciousness, coma, or vegetative state. There is no reason why you cannot use both the living will and the power of attorney for health care, though it is important for them to be consistent with each other.

While living wills and health care powers of attorney are often offered to the patient as part of the hospital admission procedure, they are not adequately explained or reviewed. These documents are much more effective if executed at a time when you are able to calmly and rationally provide the necessary guidance to your family. Moreover, depending on your condition at the time of such admission, you may not be in a position to execute the documents at all.

The Illinois power of attorney for health care is too long to set forth fully in this book. However, on the next page is an excerpt from the form that sets forth the powers given to a health care agent unless restricted elsewhere in the form. On the following page is the form of living will used in Illinois, which contains language typical of such forms.

The advance health care directives currently in effect for every jurisdiction are available at the website of Choices in Dying: www.choices.org. This website also summarizes recent legislation and discusses the ethical and legal problems involving the cessation of life.

Excerpt From The Illinois Statutory Short Form Power of Attorney for Health Care

...the statutory health care power shall include the following powers, subject to any limitations appearing on the face of the form:

(1) The agent is authorized to give consent to and authorize or refuse, or to withhold or withdraw consent to, any and all types of medical care, treatment or procedures relating to the physical or mental health of the principal, including any medication program, surgical procedures, life-sustaining treatment or provision of food and fluids for the principal.

(2) The agent is authorized to admit the principal to or discharge the principal from any and all types of hospitals, institutions, homes, residential or nursing facilities, treatment centers and other health care institutions providing personal care or treatment for any type of physical or mental condition. The agent shall have the same right to visit the principal in the hospital or other institution as is granted to a spouse or adult child of the principal, any rule of the institution to the contrary notwithstanding.

(3) The agent is authorized to contract for any and all types of health care services and facilities in the name of and on behalf of the principal and to bind the principal to pay for all such services and facilities, and to have and exercise those powers over the principal's property as are authorized under the statutory property power, to the extent the agent deems necessary to pay health care costs; and the agent shall not be personally liable for any services or care contracted for or on behalf of the principal.

(4) At the principal's expense and subject to reasonable rules of the health care provider to prevent disruption of the principal's health care, the agent shall have the same right the principal has to examine and copy and consent to disclosure of all the principal's medical records that the agent deems relevant to the exercise of the agent's powers, whether the records relate to mental health or any other medical condition and whether they are in the possession of or maintained by any physician, psychiatrist, psychologist, therapist, hospital, nursing home or other health care provider.

(5) The agent is authorized: to direct that an autopsy be made pursuant to Section 2 of "An Act in relation to autopsy of dead bodies," approved August 13, 1965, including all amendments; to make a disposition of any part or all of the principal's body pursuant to the Uniform Anatomical Gift Act, as now or hereafter amended; and to direct the disposition of the principal's remains.

Living Will

This declaration is made this ____ day of _____, ____. I, _____, being of legal age and sound mind, willfully and voluntarily make known my desires that my moment of death shall not be artificially postponed.

If at any time I should have an incurable and irreversible injury, disease, or illness judged to be a terminal condition by my attending physician who has personally examined me and has determined that my death is imminent except for death delaying procedures, I direct that such procedures which would only prolong the dying process be withheld or withdrawn, and that I be permitted to die naturally with only the administration of medication, sustenance, or the performance of any medical procedure deemed necessary by my attending physician to provide me with comfort care.

In the absence of my ability to give directions regarding the use of such death delaying procedures, it is my intention that this declaration shall be honored by my family and physician as the final expression of my legal right to refuse medical or surgical treatment and accept the consequences from such refusal.

Signed: _____

City, County and State of Residence: _____

_____

Chapter 9
The Transfer Tax System

In planning your estate, it is essential to have a clear understanding of *transfer taxes*, which include *death taxes*, *gift taxes*, and *generation-skipping taxes*. We will begin with a discussion of death taxes, the largest component of which is the *federal estate tax*, to which all citizens and residents are subject. In addition, each of the states imposes either an *estate tax* or an *inheritance tax*.

State Death Taxes

Every state imposes an estate tax equal to a credit allowed by the federal estate tax system for state death taxes, which is a percentage computed on a sliding scale. If they did not, the credit would not be allowed and the decedent would have to pay the credit amount to the federal government. In other words, the states are accepting a hand out from the federal government of a portion of the federal estate tax. This tax is usually referred to as the *pick-up tax*, because it is there to be "picked up" by the states.

The pick-up tax is the only death tax imposed by most states. However, a number of states also charge a separate estate or inheritance tax. An estate tax is charged against the decedent's estate as a whole. An inheritance tax is computed on each individual inheritance received from the decedent. Inheritance tax rates typically vary depending on how closely the individual is related to the decedent. In most states that have a separate tax, that tax is separately computed, with the estate then being required to pay the larger of the pick-up tax or the separate tax.

Because Illinois is among the majority of the states that charge only the pick-up tax, for purposes of the following discussion I will deal only with the gross federal estate tax, which is the total of the net federal estate tax and the Illinois estate tax. For convenience, this total amount will be referred to as the federal estate tax or, simply, the estate tax.

The Federal Estate Tax

The federal estate tax is computed on the value of all assets in which the decedent had an interest at death. After totaling the value of the *gross estate*, certain deductions are allowed in arriving at the amount of the *taxable estate*.

Property Includible in Gross Estate

There are many misconceptions about what is taxable for estate tax purposes. The following is by no means an exhaustive list of what is and is not taxable, but it includes the types of property owned by most people:

Property Held in Sole Ownership

Property held in the decedent's sole ownership (including property held in tenancy in common) is included in the gross estate.

Property Held in Joint Tenancy

Joint tenancy property between a husband and wife is 50% included in the deceased spouse's gross estate. For estate tax purposes this is of no consequence, because transfers between spouses are non-taxable. (In fact, it would be better if the property were 100% included, because then the surviving joint tenant would receive a fully stepped-up basis for income tax purposes, as will be discussed in Chapter 11.)

Joint tenancy property among persons not married to one another is included in the decedent's gross estate in proportion to the decedent's contribution toward the property. The Internal Revenue Code assumes that the deceased joint tenant provided all of the contribution toward the property. The burden of proof then shifts to the decedent's estate to prove otherwise. This is one of the reasons that I do not recommend the use of joint tenancy by persons not married to one another.

Life Insurance

I am always surprised at the number of people who believe that life insurance passes free of estate taxes. Life insurance proceeds do pass free of income taxes, but they do not pass free of estate taxes unless ownership of the policy has been irrevocably transferred, as will be discussed in considerable detail in Chapters 19 and 20. For now, remember that the proceeds of a life insurance policy on a decedent's life that was owned by the decedent are fully included in the decedent's gross estate.

Qualified Retirement Plans and IRAs

Retirement plans are fully included in the plan participant's gross estate.

Annuities

If there is a death benefit payable by an annuity following the annuitant's death, that death benefit will generally be included in the gross estate. Many annuities, by design, pay out only over the annuitant's lifetime, in which case there is generally no residual value to be included in the gross estate.

Property Held in Trust

If a person creates a trust and retains virtually any control over or benefit from the trust property, the property is included in that person's gross estate at death. There is no magic trust that permits the trust's creator lifetime access to the trust funds, yet avoids the estate tax, as many of my clients would like to believe.

If the decedent was a beneficiary of a trust created by someone else, the includibility of the trust in the decedent's gross estate depends on the exact terms of that trust. If the trust was established by the beneficiary's predeceased spouse, and if it qualified for the marital deduction when that spouse died, it will be included in the surviving spouse's gross estate. Most other trusts will not be included in the beneficiary's gross estate unless the draftsman gave the beneficiary, deliberately or otherwise, overly-broad powers of control over the disposition of the trust property.

Deductions

Once the value of the gross estate has been calculated, the next step is to claim all of the deductions allowed by the Internal Revenue Code.

Debts

A decedent's estate is entitled to deduct all amounts owed by the decedent at the time of his or her death. This includes mortgages owed on any properties included in the estate, accrued real estate taxes, credit card debt, utility bills, medical expenses, etc.

Administration Expenses

All of the fees and expenses necessary to administer the decedent's affairs after death are deductible in this category. This includes attorneys' and accountants' fees, executors' and trustees' fees, and funeral and burial expenses. The costs of selling assets are also deductible, but only to the extent that the sale of an asset is reasonably required for the administration of the estate.

Most administration expenses can be deducted on either the federal estate tax return or the income tax return for the estate or trust, but not both. Good post-mortem tax planning dictates that they be deducted where they will save the most money, which is determined by comparing the marginal estate and income tax rates.

The Marital Deduction

Probably the single most important deduction is the marital deduction, because it permits transfers between spouses to pass free of estate taxes. The marital deduction is allowed for transfers ranging from an outright bequest to a bequest in trust from which the surviving spouse receives only the income for life. The marital deduction in unlimited in amount.

It is important to understand that even though the marital deduction avoids taxes at the first death, the assets remaining at the surviving spouse's death are subject to estate taxes. Therefore, the marital deduction should be thought of as a means of deferring taxes, not avoiding them. The marital deduction is covered in more detail in Chapter 12.

An important note: If either you or your spouse is not a United States citizen, it is important that your estate planner know this. When the surviving spouse is a non-citizen, the decedent's estate plan must create what is known as a *qualified domestic trust*, or *QDOT*, in order for the amount passing to the surviving spouse to qualify for the marital deduction.

The Charitable Deduction

Unlike the income tax system, which limits the amount of the charitable deduction that can be taken in any one year, the estate tax charitable deduction is unlimited. For those determined to avoid death taxes altogether, this deduction can provide the means. The charitable deduction will be more thoroughly covered in Chapter 22.

Exemption and Calculation

Once the *taxable estate* has been determined, by subtracting all allowable deductions from the gross estate, the estate tax is calculated. I won't bore you with the details of this computation, which is convoluted in only a way that the IRS could dream up. What effectively happens is that the estate is allowed an exemption from the tax. (Technically, there is no such exemption, but the term is in such common usage, and so accurately describes the calculation method, I will use the term exemption throughout this book.)

As of 1999 the estate tax exemption is $650,000, but it is scheduled to increase so that by 2006 the exemption will be $1,000,000. The following table shows the historical and currently projected exemption amounts.

The Estate Tax Exemption

Year	Exemption
1997	$600,000
1998	$625,000
1999	$650,000
2000	$675,000
2001	$675,000
2002	$700,000
2003	$700,000
2004	$850,000
2005	$950,000
2006 and after	$1,000,000

Once the exemption is allowed, the tax on the balance of the taxable estate is based on a rate schedule. The rate schedule is a progressive one. The first dollar over the $650,000 exemption

Estate Tax Calculator

Taxable Estate	1999	2001	2000 2003	2002 2004	2005	2006 and later	Rate on Excess
$ 650,000	$ -0-	$ -0-	$ -0-	$ -0-	$ -0-	$ -0-	37%
750,000	37,000	27,750	18,500	-0-	-0-	-0-	39%
1,000,000	134,500	125,250	116,000	58,500	19,500	-0-	41%
1,250,000	237,000	227,750	218,500	161,000	122,000	102,500	43%
1,500,000	344,500	335,250	326,000	268,500	229,500	210,000	45%
2,000,000	569,500	560,250	551,000	493,500	454,500	435,000	49%
2,500,000	814,500	805,250	796,000	738,500	699,500	680,000	53%
3,000,000	1,079,500	1,070,250	1,061,000	1,003,500	964,500	945,000	55%
10,000,000	4,929,500	4,920,250	4,911,000	4,853,500	4,814,500	4,795,000	60%
21,040,000	11,553,500	11,544,250	11,535,000	11,477,500	11,438,500	11,419,000	55%

Assume an estate of $2,300,000 and a death in 2006. The tax is $435,000 plus 49% of the excess over $2,000,000, or $435,000 + $147,000, or $582,000. Assume a married couple with combined assets of $2,300,000 with the first death in 2003 and the second death occurring in or after 2006. First, subtract the $700,000 exemption available at the first death, resulting in the surviving spouse having $1,600,000. The tax at the second death will be $210,000 plus 45% of the excess over $1,500,000, or $210,000 + $45,000, or $255,000. As explained in the text, the estate taxes computed in this table include the state death taxes charged by most states, including Illinois.

amount is taxed at 37% and the top marginal rate is 55% (although amounts over $10,000,000 are taxed at 60% until the entire estate is taxed at a flat 55% rate, which occurs when the estate reaches $21,040,000).

The table on the preceding page illustrates the tax rates and the total taxes at various estate values. This table shows that once an estate exceeds the exemption amount, the government imposes a significant tax on the excess. People in this situation are well-advised to take appropriate steps to reduce or defer this tax.

The Federal Gift Tax

The federal estate tax would not be very effective if a person could simply give away property during lifetime and avoid its effect. Therefore, since 1932, there has been a federal gift tax imposed on lifetime transfers. Prior to 1977, the transfer tax system favored lifetime transfers, for the tax imposed on gifts was only 75% of the tax imposed on transfers at death.

Today, the Internal Revenue Code is structured so that the gift tax and the estate tax are combined into a single transfer tax system —the *unified transfer tax*. The two taxes within this unified structure are very similar:

- The tax rate is the same for both the gift and estate taxes.

- The gift and estate taxes use the same exemption. To the extent this exemption is used during lifetime, it is unavailable at death.

- The gift tax is calculated based on total gifts made, while the estate tax is based on total assets available for transfer.

- Like the estate tax, gifts to a spouse qualify for an unlimited marital deduction.

- Like the estate tax, gifts to charity qualify for an unlimited charitable deduction.

However, there are some differences between the estate and gift taxes. Unlike the estate tax, there is an annual *gift tax exclusion* available with respect to each separate donee. This permits the donor to exclude up to $10,000 of any gifts made to an individual each year. A separate $10,000 exclusion is available with respect to an unlimited number of gift recipients. In order to qualify, the gift must be a *present interest*, which generally means that the donee must be able to immediately own, control, and enjoy the entire gift. The $10,000 annual gift tax exclusion is a significant estate planning technique that will be discussed in more detail in Chapter 17.

Effective with the Taxpayer Relief Act of 1997, the annual gift tax exclusion is indexed to inflation, but will change only in $1,000 increments. It is currently estimated that the gift tax exclusion will change from $10,000 to $11,000 in the year 2000.

The following example illustrates how the gift and estate taxes work together:

> Assume that Sam—a widower—makes an outright gift of $50,000 to each of his four children this year. There will be an exclusion of $10,000 with respect to each gift, but $40,000 of each gift will be taxable. These four gifts will therefore use up $160,000 of his exemption. If Sam dies in 2003, when the exemption will be $700,000, and has made no further taxable gifts, only $540,000 of his exemption will remain to offset the estate taxes on his estate.

Because the $10,000 annual gift tax exclusion applies to each donor, a married couple can make $20,000 of annual gifts to as many persons as they desire without using any part of their respective exemptions. This is accomplished in one of two ways:

- Each spouse can give $10,000 from his or her own funds to each donee. Assuming no taxable gifts are made during the year, no gift tax return will have to be filed.

- Even if one spouse gives away more than $10,000 to any one donee, the couple can elect to treat the gift as if it were made 50% by each of them. This is known as *gift-splitting*. Each spouse must file a gift tax return in order to make this election, even if the end result is that there are no taxable gifts.

There are two other gift tax exclusions in addition to the $10,000 annual exclusion of which you should be aware:

- Any tuition payments made to a qualified educational institution for the education or training of the donee are excluded for gift tax purposes, without limitation. The payment must be made directly to the institution and not to the donee in order to qualify for the exclusion. Room, board, and book expenses are not part of the tuition exclusion.

- Any payments made directly to the provider of medical services with respect to the medical care of the donee are also excluded for gift tax purposes. It is not acceptable to reimburse someone who has already made such payments; the payments must be made directly to the doctor, hospital, or other provider.

As previously noted, a gift qualifying for the $10,000 annual exclusion must be a present interest in property and is typically made outright to the donee. However, there are two exceptions to this general rule:

- A gift made to a child under the age of 21 may be put into a trust known as a §2503(c) trust. Such a trust is permitted to accumulate income for the future benefit of the child, so long as the child is given the right at age 21 to withdraw all of the money in the trust. The §2503(c) trust is discussed in detail in Chapter 18.

- A gift to a trust from which a donee is given the immediate opportunity to withdraw the contributed amount can also qualify as a present interest. This technique, known as a Crummey power (after the name of the Supreme Court case in which it was first permitted), is discussed in more detail in Chapter 20.

Most states, including Illinois, do not levy a gift tax. Because of the way in which the state death tax credit is computed, they eventually receive their fair share of the total federal transfer taxes. Some states, usually those with a separate inheritance tax, do levy a gift tax.

Summary

I have felt it necessary to provide quite a bit of detail in this chapter. Considering that multi-volume treatises have been written on the subject of estate taxes, this chapter is blessedly brief. The contents of the box on the following page are an attempt to condense the topic even more, highlighting the key concepts you should take away from this chapter.

A Summary of the Federal Estate and Gift Tax System

- You can give $10,000 per year to as many persons as you desire. All such gifts will be excluded for tax purposes.

- Any lifetime gifts in excess of the excluded amounts are taxable, but are offset by your transfer tax exemption, which is $650,000 in 1999.

- Lifetime gifts in excess of the exclusion and exemption amounts will be taxed, beginning at a 37% rate.

- Upon death, the taxable estate is determined by adding together all property in which the decedent had an interest, then subtracting debts, administration expenses, and the value of all property passing to the surviving spouse or charity.

- The transfer tax exemption not used during lifetime will reduce the amount subject to tax, but amounts in excess of the exemption will be taxed, using the same rate schedule as for gifts.

Chapter 10
The Estate Tax Shelter Trust

Without question, the most effective estate planning technique for most married couples is the estate tax shelter trust. Any couple with combined assets in excess of the estate tax exemption amount that does not utilize this technique is missing a simple and easy way to save a significant amount of estate taxes—as much as $357,500 at current tax rates.

The estate tax shelter trust technique makes use of both the estate tax exemption and the unlimited marital deduction to defer and minimize the estate tax. The technique is explained in this chapter, but you will need to read the following two chapters for a full appreciation of how it is implemented.

How the Estate Tax Shelter Trust Works

Let's look at the estate plan of Jim and Janet. This couple has total assets of $1,700,000. Jim has securities, cash, and life insurance of $1,300,000, Janet has assets of $100,000, and the couple's $300,000 residence is held in joint tenancy. If Jim dies in 1999 and leaves his entire estate to Janet, either by the terms of his will or trust, by beneficiary designation, or through joint tenancy, there will be no tax payable at his death because of the unlimited marital deduction. However, when Janet dies in, for example, 2006, owning an estate still valued at $1,700,000, a tax of $300,000 will be payable because her then available estate tax exemption can only shelter $1,000,000. If she dies earlier, even more tax will be payable.

Proper planning avoids almost all of this tax. The tax occurs because no use is made of Jim's available exemption of $650,000 from the estate tax. Suppose that instead of leaving his entire estate to Janet, Jim's estate plan establishes what we will call an *estate tax shelter trust*. The trust will be created and funded at Jim's death, with an amount equal to the estate tax exemption amount available to Jim's estate at the time of his death.

Assume that Jim dies in 1999. The recommended estate plan provides that $650,000 will be allocated to the estate tax shelter trust, with the rest passing to Janet or into a marital deduction trust for her benefit. Jim's estate still passes free of tax. The shelter trust is non-taxable because of Jim's $650,000 exemption, and the balance of the estate is non-taxable because of the marital deduction.

At Janet's subsequent death, the property set aside in the shelter trust—regardless of its value at her death—is not includible in her estate for estate tax purposes. To accomplish this the shelter trust must be properly worded, *i.e.*, it must contain certain technical restrictions on Janet's access to the trust funds. These restrictions will be discussed in detail in Chapter 12, but for now be assured that these restrictions impose no significant impediment to Janet's full use of the funds in the shelter trust during her lifetime.

Therefore, even though Janet has virtually full access to the couple's total assets of $1,700,000, only $1,050,000 will be taxable for estate tax purposes at her subsequent death, an amount that can be almost completely sheltered by her then available $1,000,000 exemption. The tax payable at Janet's death in this example is only $20,500, which is $279,500 less than the tax without the estate tax shelter trust. A simple estate planning technique saves the couple's descendants more than a quarter-million dollars in estate taxes. There is a diagram of Jim's and Janet's estate plans, with and without this technique, on the following page.

The technique is useful, in theory, for any estate where the combined assets of a couple exceed the currently available exemption. For example, assuming combined assets of $750,000 (after payment of debts and administration expenses), a tax of $37,000

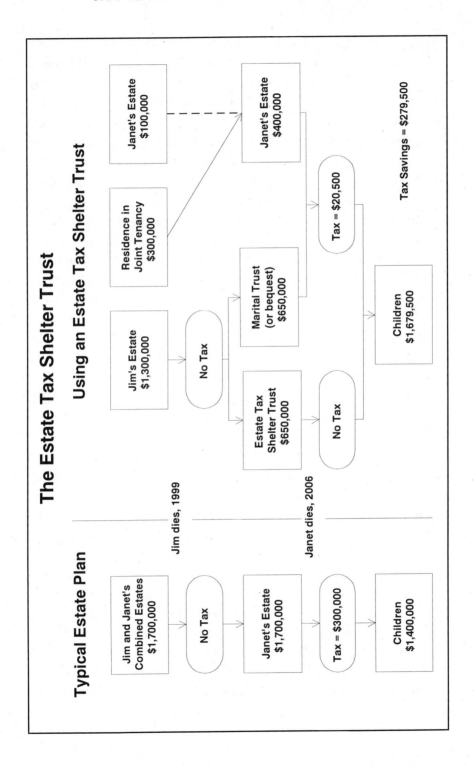

The Estate Tax Shelter Trust

Typical Estate Plan

Using an Estate Tax Shelter Trust

Jim and Janet's Combined Estates $1,700,000

No Tax

Jim dies, 1999

Janet's Estate $1,700,000

Tax = $300,000

Janet dies, 2006

Children $1,400,000

Janet's Estate $100,000

Residence in Joint Tenancy $300,000

Jim's Estate $1,300,000

No Tax

Marital Trust (or bequest) $650,000

Estate Tax Shelter Trust $650,000

Janet's Estate $400,000

Tax = $20,500

No Tax

Children $1,679,500

Tax Savings = $279,500

would be payable at the surviving spouse's death in 1999 if the technique is not used, while no tax would be due if the technique is used. The savings available from this technique ranges from 37% to 55% of the available exemption. At the 1999 exemption level of $650,000, the maximum tax savings is $357,500. At the $1,000,000 exemption level, which will be reached in 2006, the potential tax savings is $550,000, with the estate tax shelter trust technique able to protect a total of $2,000,000 from taxation.

Even though these tax reductions are significant, the foregoing actually understates the potential savings from this plan. Significant earnings and growth can occur between the deaths of the two spouses. Once the shelter trust is created at the first death, the trust is fully tax-exempt at the second death, no matter how large it may grow in the interim period. For this reason, the surviving spouse is well-advised to spend his or her own assets, or any marital trust assets, before utilizing any of the income or principal of the shelter trust. In our previous example, if Janet spends down her own personal assets while allowing the shelter trust to grow in value, there is a high probability that her estate will entirely avoid the estate tax if she lives any reasonable length of time after Jim's death.

To illustrate, assume Jim and Janet both live until 2006, when their combined assets are now $2,500,000. Jim dies, allocating $1,000,000 to his estate tax shelter trust and leaving his remaining assets to Janet, who now possesses a personal estate of $1,500,000. If Janet leaves the estate tax shelter trust alone, and lives solely off of her personal assets, it is entirely possible that over time her personal (taxable) estate will be reduced below the exemption amount, while the estate tax shelter trust will have significantly increased in value. Notwithstanding this growth, the shelter trust is still fully exempt from estate taxes at Janet's death. For example, if the shelter trust grows from $1,000,000 to $1,500,000, while Janet spends down her personal assets from $1,500,000 to $1,000,000, the use of this technique will save their children a total of $680,000.

Reverse Order of Deaths

Special consideration should also be given to the situation in which the spouses die in reverse order. In the preceding example, most of the assets were owned by Jim or were held in joint tenancy. If Janet dies first, Jim will own almost the entire estate, which would then be subject to a large estate tax at his subsequent death. However, if the couple split their property so that each owns assets at least equal to the current exemption amount, the spouse who dies first can set up a fully-funded shelter trust, creating a situation in which the least tax possible will be paid by the family no matter which spouse dies first.

Another Example

Remember Henry and Helen from Chapter 1? You may recall that they had $1,200,000 of assets upon Henry's death in 1999. Because Henry left his entire estate to Helen, either by the terms of his will, through joint tenancy, or by beneficiary designation, there was no estate tax payable at his death because of the marital deduction. However, when Helen died in 2003, owning an estate then valued at $1,500,000, a tax of $326,000 was payable because the exemption available to her estate could only shelter $700,000.

Using the estate tax shelter trust technique would have avoided this tax entirely. First, because there was no way of knowing who would die first, Henry and Helen should have divided their estate so that each owned $600,000, with none of their property held in joint tenancy. When Henry died, his estate plan should have provided that his entire estate (since it was less than the estate tax exemption) be allocated to his estate tax shelter trust. Because all of Henry's assets would have been in the shelter trust, there would have been no marital trust or bequest.

You may recall that Helen's assets increased in value by a total of $300,000. By paying attention to the asset allocation between the surviving spouse's personal assets and the assets in the shelter trust,

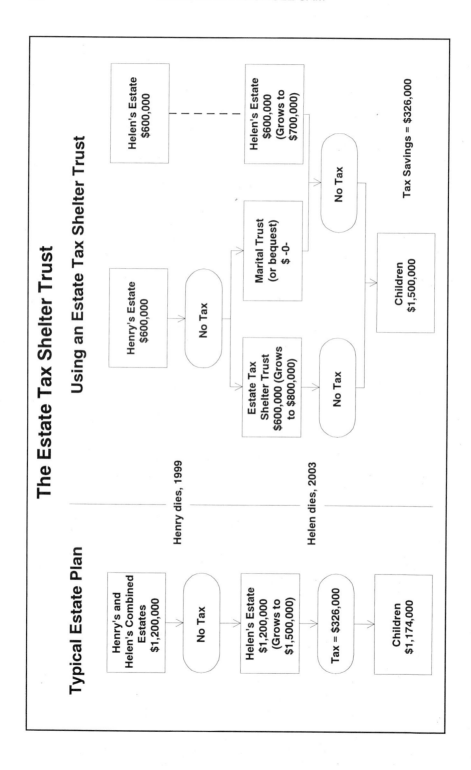

The Estate Tax Shelter Trust

Typical Estate Plan

Using an Estate Tax Shelter Trust

it is possible to have all or most of this appreciation occur inside the shelter trust. In Helen's case, however, putting the house into the shelter trust would have meant that upon its sale during Helen's lifetime, a tax of as much as $20,000 would have been payable on the $100,000 capital gain at sale. Besides, since Helen's personal assets were only $600,000, and the estate tax exemption was increasing, it was unlikely that the appreciation in the value of the house would cause her estate to exceed the exemption amount, particularly if she used her cash assets for her living expenses.

Based on the facts of the example in Chapter 1, this is exactly what happens. Upon Helen's death both the shelter trust (now increased to $800,000) and Helen's assets (now $700,000, which equals the available exemption at her death) pass to the children free of estate taxes. By using the estate tax shelter trust technique, the couple saves their children $326,000. The diagram on the preceding page illustrates this example.

The Marital Bequest

As discussed in the preceding chapter, a marital deduction is allowed for property passing directly to the surviving spouse or into a marital deduction trust for his or her benefit. Direct bequests may include property passing by joint tenancy, a beneficiary designation, or an outright distribution in a will or trust. Many couples prefer to establish marital deduction trusts, either to provide the surviving spouse with assistance in managing the trust property or so that each spouse can be sure that the property will pass to the desired beneficiaries upon the surviving spouse's death. The parameters of drafting the marital trust are covered in detail in Chapter 12.

The Estate Tax Shelter Trust

The estate tax shelter trust can take a variety of forms. Like a marital deduction trust, it can be a trust of which only the surviving spouse is beneficiary. Alternatively, it can be a trust of which both the surviving spouse and the couple's descendants are beneficiaries, with the trustee given the discretion to make income or principal distributions among them. It can also be a trust from which the surviving spouse derives no benefit, but which is solely for descendants or other family members.

Let me again stress that even though the shelter trust must be drafted in a legally restrictive manner so as not be taxed at the surviving spouse's death, in practice the trust can permit the surviving spouse almost as much control and use of the trust property as if he or she owned it outright. This will be covered in more detail in Chapter 12.

What's in a Name?

The estate tax shelter trust technique is one rose that smells as sweet under a variety of names. The use of a shelter trust in conjunction with a marital trust is often referred to as a *marital-residuary trust plan* or an *A-B trust plan*. The shelter trust is also called the *credit shelter trust, bypass trust, tax-exempt trust, residuary trust, family trust* or *B Trust*. The names used are unimportant—the tax savings are the same.

Disclaimers

There is a post-death method of saving estate taxes even if the first spouse has not created an estate tax shelter trust. The surviving spouse can *disclaim* a portion of the deceased spouse's estate, allowing it to pass to (usually) the children. Such a *disclaimer*, if signed within nine months after the first spouse's death, will not be considered a gift by the surviving spouse. The disclaimer must follow very specific rules set forth in the Internal Revenue Code. In particular, the disclaimed property must pass to those persons who would have received the property if the surviving spouse died first.

A disclaimer takes advantage of otherwise unused exemption, thus reducing the size of the surviving spouse's estate. However, the surviving spouse will not have the use of the disclaimed assets, which would have been the case if an estate tax shelter trust had been employed. It has also been my experience that spouses are very reluctant to disclaim assets unless the estate is very large. Disclaimers can be useful, but they are no substitute for a carefully planned estate.

Chapter 11
The Ownership of Property—Part Two

Incorporating an estate tax shelter trust into your and your spouse's estate planning documents doesn't guarantee tax savings. It is essential that your assets are owned in a way that the plan works properly. This chapter will revisit the topic of ownership of property first discussed in Chapter 2, but specifically for a couple wishing to use the estate tax shelter trust technique.

The Problem With Joint Tenancy

Joint tenancy assets are not governed by the will or trust of the first joint tenant to die—they pass directly to the surviving spouse at death notwithstanding the will or trust provisions. The result of owning most or all of a couple's assets in joint tenancy is that the first spouse to die will not have assets sufficient to fund the shelter trust. In order to pass into the shelter trust, property must be owned in the decedent's own name or in the name of decedent's living trust, or must be made payable to the estate or the living trust by a beneficiary designation.

The other problem with joint tenancy is that it may not be fully effective in avoiding probate. It is true that upon the death of one joint tenant the property passes to the surviving joint tenant without probate. However, if the joint tenants die simultaneously, the property passes 50% through each joint tenant's probate estate. Also, if the surviving spouse dies shortly after the first spouse, there may not have been the time to transfer the joint tenancy assets into the surviving spouse's trust, thus requiring a probate of the second estate. With few exceptions, couples with combined assets subject to estate taxes valued in excess of the exemption amount should do away with most or all of their joint tenancy holdings and own their property separately.

Many couples prefer to keep their day-to-day checking account in joint tenancy. So long as this account does not carry balances in excess of the small estate affidavit limitation ($50,000 in Illinois), this should not be a problem.

Allocation of Assets Between Spouses

If both members of a couple are using the estate tax shelter trust technique, it is important that they split their assets between them so that, no matter who dies first, the decedent will have sufficient assets to fully fund the shelter trust. For couples with total assets valued at less than $1,300,000, there will not be sufficient assets to fully accomplish this. If we knew who would be the first to die, that spouse would own a full $650,000, with the other spouse owning the balance. Of course, we usually do not know this, so the best bet is to split the assets equally. If it becomes evident who will die first, good tax planning would suggest that enough assets be transferred to the dying spouse (or his or her trust) so that he or she has property equal to the then current estate tax exemption amount.

There is another advantage to shifting assets into the ownership of the first spouse to die, if possible. Assets owned by a decedent receive a new *cost basis* for income tax purposes equal to the federal estate tax value of the assets. This is frequently referred to as a *stepped-up basis*. Stepped-up basis at death is only achieved if the transfer was made more than one year prior to death. Deathbed planning will not achieve this particular tax savings.

Assume a person bought stock at $10 per share that is now worth $100 per share. If the stock were sold during lifetime, there would be a capital gain of $90 per share. However, if the stock is retained until death and then sold by the estate or a beneficiary, the capital gain is computed based on the difference between the sales price and the federal estate tax value (usually the value on the decedent's date of death). This represents a significant savings, and suggests that older individuals should retain highly-appreciated securities until death to achieve a stepped-up basis for their estates. However, beware of letting tax considerations prevail over sound investment decisions—it may not be worth saving the 20% maximum capital gains tax if the result is retaining securities that are not performing well.

Ownership of the Residence

One asset that presents a special set of concerns is the marital residence. Most couples own this asset in joint tenancy with right of survivorship or tenancy by the entireties, as discussed in Chapter 2. However, in order to divide the couple's assets between them, it is frequently necessary to assign ownership of the residence to one or the other's living trust (or, occasionally, to split ownership between the trusts).

Some people like the idea of owning their residence jointly because they want to own their home if their spouse dies—there is a certain feeling of security associated with home ownership. Yet the residence is an ideal asset to be placed into the estate tax shelter trust. The surviving spouse can continue to live in the home if it is in trust just as easily as if it is titled in his or her name. If the surviving spouse wants to sell the residence, the trust can sell it and buy a new one, or can retain the sales proceeds in the trust for the benefit of the surviving spouse. Most importantly, a residence usually grows in value, which means that this appreciation will also pass free of estate taxes on the surviving spouse's death.

The only significant disadvantage of the shelter trust owning the residence is the loss of the exemption from capital gains tax. The 1997 tax act expanded the exemption from capital gains tax on the sale of a personal residence to $250,000 per person ($500,000 per couple). To the extent the estate tax shelter trust owns the home, this exemption is not available. However, keep in mind that because the residence has passed through a decedent's estate to get into the shelter trust, the cost basis of the property is stepped up to the federal estate tax value as of the deceased spouse's death. Therefore, if the residence is sold quickly, there will be no gain. Even if the home is sold much later, and some gain is incurred, the maximum capital gains rate is 20%. The same appreciation would be taxed at between 37%-55% for estate tax purposes if it were not in the shelter trust.

If there are sufficient other assets that can be divided between the spouses so that whoever is the first to die can fully fund an estate tax shelter trust, the residence should be retained in joint ownership. (Upon the death of either, the surviving spouse should promptly transfer ownership of any inherited joint property to his or her living trust to avoid probate on his or her subsequent death). However, if the other assets are not sufficient, I generally recommend that the residence be owned by one spouse or the other— preferably in trust—so that it is available to fund that spouse's shelter trust, notwithstanding the possible exposure to capital gains taxes.

Designations of Beneficiary

It is important for spouses to carefully scrutinize the beneficiary designations on their life insurance and retirement plans, with the goal that each spouse should have, if possible, enough to fully fund the shelter trust ($650,000 in 1999).

Life Insurance

As described in Chapter 19, life insurance owned by the insured should be payable to the insured's trust: "The acting trustee of the [name of insured's trust] dated [date of trust]," *e.g.*, "The acting trustee of the Helen E. Doe Trust dated December 19, 1998." Any such life insurance should be counted when determining whether that spouse has $650,000 of assets in his or her separate ownership.

Retirement Plans

The question of how qualified retirement plans and IRAs should be payable at death can be extremely complicated. I have written the longest chapter of this book in an effort to present a "simplified" explanation of this topic. Chapter 21 should be studied before a final decision is made with respect to beneficiary designations of retirement plans, with particular attention to the decision tree near the end of that chapter. Most people will name beneficiaries as follows:

- Married couples will usually want to name one another as the primary beneficiary of their retirement plans, even though it means underfunding the estate tax shelter trust, so that a *spousal rollover* can be made. The secondary beneficiary should usually be the trustees of their living trusts. For example:

  Primary beneficiary: My wife, Helen E. Doe

  Secondary beneficiary: The acting trustee of the Henry A. Doe Trust dated December 19, 1998.

- Single individuals will usually name the trustees of their living trusts as the beneficiary.

- Roth IRAs should generally be made payable to the trustee or trustees of the living trust.

It is essential that any such beneficiary designation be carefully reviewed by the time the person attains age 70½—and possibly changed—for reasons discussed in Chapter 21.

Why do I recommend a beneficiary designation for a married couple that may result in the estate tax shelter trust being under-funded? Retirement plan proceeds payable to a shelter trust are taxable for income tax purposes and can no longer earn income on a tax-deferred basis. However, if the plan is payable to the surviving spouse it can be rolled over income tax free to an IRA and continue to enjoy tax-deferred status. This will be more fully explained in Chapter 21.

The following diagram illustrates the flow of assets at death when using a living trust and appropriate beneficiary designations.

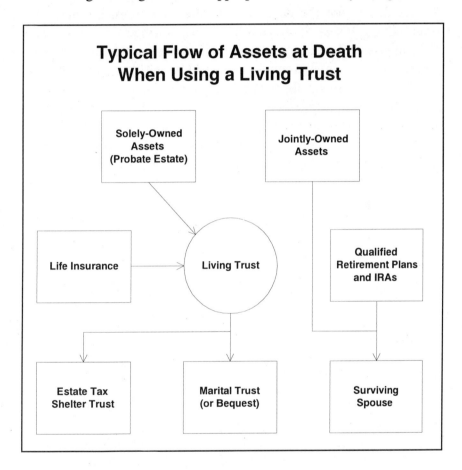

A Word of Caution

One of the problems with lifetime transfers between spouses for estate planning purposes is how such transfers will be treated upon a divorce. The issue is a complicated one because of the interrelationship of property law, probate law, and the law relating to the dissolution of marriage. In Illinois, property given by one spouse to the other is generally treated as becoming the *separate property* of the donee spouse. This would mean that upon a later divorce, the donee spouse would own that asset free and clear.

As this is not the desired result for most transfers made for estate tax purposes, many couples wish to change this result. This is accomplished by the couple entering into a post-nuptial agreement as part of the estate planning process in which they agree that the transfers being made for estate tax purposes will not change the nature of the property. For example, if the gifted property is *marital property*, which is subject to division upon divorce, the couple can agree that it will remain as marital property even if titled in the name of only one of the spouses (or his or her trust).

Summary of Asset Ownership and Beneficiary Designations for Couples Using Living Trusts and the Estate Tax Shelter Trust Technique

- Assets should be separately-owned so that each spouse has, if there are sufficient assets, the amount of the currently available exemption ($650,000 in 1999). Separately-owned means sole ownership in each spouse's name or, preferably, ownership in each spouse's living trust.

- Assets in excess of the exemption amount can be owned separately or in joint ownership—it makes no difference for estate tax purposes. If the residence is among these assets it should be owned jointly; to be sure of probate avoidance, the remaining assets should be owned separately in one or the other's trust. There is an income tax advantage if highly-appreciated assets are separately-owned by the spouse (or that spouse's trust) who is most likely to die first.

- Life insurance (unless it is to be removed from the taxable estate using the techniques discussed in Chapters 19 and 20) should be payable to the acting trustee of the insured's trust.

- Qualified retirement plans (including IRAs, but not the Roth IRA) should be payable to the surviving spouse, as primary beneficiary, and, until the plan participant is nearing or over age 70½, to the plan participant's living trust, as secondary beneficiary.

Chapter 12
Drafting for the Surviving Spouse

While most people like the tax savings they achieve by using the estate tax shelter trust technique, they are sometimes uneasy about the use of a trust. They fear that the surviving spouse will lose control over the property placed in that trust.

The Estate Tax Shelter Trust

To allay those fears, let's start with a discussion of the drafting of the shelter trust. Keep in mind that this trust must be carefully constructed so that it will not be included in the surviving spouse's estate, particularly if the surviving spouse is acting as trustee or co-trustee at his or her death. A good clue to the experience level of your estate planner is whether or not he or she is willing to draft a shelter trust which has the surviving spouse as its sole trustee. It can be done, but I am surprised at the number of attorneys who routinely advise their clients otherwise.

Payments of Income

The trustee can be required to pay all of the trust income of the shelter trust to the surviving spouse. I generally do not recommend this, for it means that regardless of the spouse's needs, income tax bracket, reliance on government programs such as Medicaid, etc., all of the income is forced out to the surviving spouse each year. Ideally, the trustee should have discretion to pay out the income or retain it, and I usually recommend that the trustee also have the right to make discretionary income payments among the couple's descendants.

As already noted, the trustee can be the surviving spouse. This comes at a price, for having the discretion to pay himself or herself all of the income means that the surviving spouse is taxable on all of the income, whether paid out or not. If this discretion is instead given to a co-trustee, the income is taxed to the surviving spouse only if distributed. Most couples decide to forego the possible income tax savings in favor of full control. A provision can be added by which the spouse acting as sole trustee may appoint a co-trustee for the purpose of exercising this discretion.

Payments of Principal

For maximum flexibility the trustee of the shelter trust should have the discretion to make principal payments to the surviving spouse, as well as to descendants, although the instrument should usually provide that the spouse's needs are paramount. As previously discussed, the shelter trust passes free of estate tax at the surviving spouse's death, but the surviving spouse's own assets and the assets of any marital trust are subject to estate taxes. Therefore, principal payments should be made to the surviving spouse from the shelter trust only if his or her taxable assets are below the current taxable threshold or if there is insufficient liquidity in the marital trust.

If the surviving spouse is acting as sole trustee, the standard under which principal distributions are made must be worded very carefully. Unless an *ascertainable standard* is used to define the trustee's discretionary power to distribute principal, the entire trust will be taxed at the spouse's death. The permitted standard includes "support" (in accustomed manner of living), "health care," and "maintenance," and combinations and some limited variations thereof.

While the ascertainable standard is considered a limited standard, remember that it is the surviving spouse who is determining his or her support, health care, and maintenance needs. The

Internal Revenue Service is not likely to challenge the spouse if the standard is violated—they prefer that the tax-sheltered dollars be spent. The spouse who exceeds the stated standards is subject to criticism by the trust *remaindermen*, usually the children and grandchildren. This is usually only a problem in second marriage situations.

Power of Appointment

I am now going to introduce you to the *power of appointment*. This estate planning tool is an excellent way to provide flexibility in an estate plan. A power of appointment is typically a right given to a trust beneficiary to designate in his or her will how the trust property will be distributed after the beneficiary's death. In the context of our present discussion, the surviving spouse can be given the power to provide in his or her will who will be the ultimate beneficiaries of the estate tax shelter trust. This provides the couple with the flexibility to delay a final decision as to the distribution of the shelter trust up until the death of the surviving spouse.

For example, if the husband dies at an unusually young age, while his children are minors, the shelter trust might not distribute to his descendants until many decades in the future. In the meantime there will be births and deaths, marriages and divorces, financial fortune and misfortune, and illness, in ways the husband cannot possibly predict while creating his estate plan. He can, however, grant to his wife the power to change the distribution of the shelter trust through a power of appointment. If she does not exercise this power, his estate plan determines how the trust assets are distributed.

Granting too broad a power of appointment to the surviving spouse will cause the inclusion of the shelter trust in the survivor's taxable estate. To avoid this inclusion, the Internal Revenue Code requires that the power not be exercisable in favor of the spouse's creditors, estate, or creditors of the estate. This is not a significant limitation. The surviving spouse can still be given the right to appoint the trust property to almost any individual or organization in the world.

This so-called *limited power of appointment* can be so broad that most couples prefer to limit the scope of the power. Many people choose to restrict the permissible beneficiaries to the couple's descendants. Often the spouses of these descendants are also included. The next step would be to permit appointment to the descendants of parents, *i.e.*, siblings and their descendants. Sometimes charitable organizations are added. The power of appointment is very flexible, and can be made as restricted or as broad as desired.

A power of appointment, however, can be a two-edged sword. I like to think that the surviving spouse will use the power to provide for the unexpected illness of a child, educational opportunities for grandchildren, or the destitute spouse of one the couple's children. However, it could be used by a cranky old beneficiary to disinherit a child or, if it is broad enough, to leave the entire trust to a charlatan preacher. While safeguards can be built into the power, every restriction on the power limits its effectiveness and flexibility.

I strongly believe in using powers of appointment wherever possible. It has been my experience that for every time they are used unwisely or vindictively, they are used wisely and generously on numerous occasions.

Sample Provision

A typical estate tax shelter trust might be worded something like this:

> **Income and Principal.** The trustee may pay to or for the benefit of my husband and my descendants so much of the income and principal as the trustee determines to be required for the beneficiary's support, health care, and education. My primary concern is for the needs of my husband. I recommend, however, that no principal payments be made to my husband while readily marketable assets remain in the Marital Trust or are otherwise available to my husband.

Distribution on Spouse's Death. On my husband's death, the trust shall be distributed to or for such one or more of my descendants and their spouses in such proportions and subject to such trusts, powers and conditions as my husband appoints by will specifically referring to this power of appointment. To the extent he does not effectively exercise this power of appointment, the trustee shall distribute the trust *per stirpes* to my then living descendants.

Is This Trust Too Restrictive?

Keeping in mind that an estate tax shelter trust has the ability to save somewhere between 37-60% of its ultimate value at the surviving spouse's death, are the following trust provisions too restrictive?

- The surviving spouse has sole authority to pay himself or herself as much of the income and principal as required for his or her accustomed manner of living and health care. The interpretation of this discretionary standard is solely the decision of the surviving spouse.

- The surviving spouse has sole investment authority over the trust property.

- At death, the surviving spouse decides who receives the trust property.

Not all estate tax shelter trusts are this liberal, but they can be. I make sure my clients have thought long and hard before they sacrifice the tax-savings available from this trust in favor of "simplicity" and "control."

The Marital Trust or Bequest

As noted in Chapter 10, there is no tax reason why the assets in excess of the exemption amount have to be placed in a trust. If desired, the first spouse to die can simply provide that all property not passing into the shelter trust is distributed outright to the surviving spouse.

However, for many reasons, there may be a desire for a marital trust. Here are some of those reasons:

- The surviving spouse is not adept at managing money and needs the assistance of a professional trustee.

- The surviving spouse is likely to squander the money.

- The person creating the trust wants to control the ultimate distribution of the trust property.

- A trust provides protection from creditors and protects the funds in the event the surviving spouse remarries, then divorces.

Let's first examine what provisions a marital trust can and cannot contain, keeping in mind that it is essential for the marital trust to qualify for the federal estate tax marital deduction.

A marital deduction is available for assets placed in trust so long as the surviving spouse receives all of the income and is the only beneficiary of the trust. He or she does not need to be given any other interest in the trust. It is an interesting anomaly of the tax code that it is possible for a trust not includible in the surviving spouse's taxable estate to be controlled and enjoyed by that spouse to a greater extent than a trust that is includible.

Using this extremely restricted marital trust as a starting point, let's examine what additional provisions can be made for the surviving spouse.

Discretionary Principal Distributions

Usually, the trustee will have the additional discretion to make principal distributions from the marital trust to the surviving spouse.

Remember, we would rather have the survivor spend a dollar from the marital trust than from the shelter trust. The discretionary standard used for principal distributions can vary from "support" all the way to "best interests" and "happiness."

Right to Withdraw Principal

The surviving spouse may also be granted the right to withdraw principal from a marital trust. Limitations can be placed on annual or aggregate withdrawals. Where my clients indicate to me they would just as soon have the marital deduction portion distributed outright, I usually establish a marital trust in the estate plan, then provide for an immediate and full right of withdrawal. This is the equivalent of an outright bequest, but gives the spouse the option of retaining the trust.

Powers of Appointment

Powers of appointment are also an effective planning tool in the marital trust. For tax purposes, there are no restrictions on the scope of the power of appointment. If the permissible appointees do not include the survivor's estate, creditors, or the creditors of the estate, the marital trust created is known as a *qualified terminable interest property trust*, or QTIP trust. In non-technical language, a QTIP trust is simply a trust as to which there is some restriction as to the surviving spouse's right to determine the ultimate recipients.

Keeping a String on the Marital Bequest

I cannot tell you the number of times I have had clients express the wish that the marital deduction portion go outright to the surviving spouse, as his or her sole property, but then later in the same meeting they tell me that they want to be sure that the property goes to the children upon the survivor's death. You cannot have it both ways. Property passing outright to the surviving spouse can be disposed of however he or she desires. Property that is restricted as to whom it can eventually pass should be restricted in a trust.

I am very much aware that there is a device known as a *joint and mutual will* that can provide for the equivalent of an outright distribution to the surviving spouse, yet require that spouse to leave the property to children. However, joint and mutual wills, and similar devices, are so easily circumvented and have engendered so much litigation over the years that I cannot recommend them as an effective estate planing device.

For those wishing freedom coupled with some restriction as to the ultimate beneficiaries, I recommend the following marital trust provisions:

• The surviving spouse is named as sole trustee.

• The surviving spouse receives all the income and may withdraw so much of the principal as he or she needs for best interests.

• The surviving spouse has a testamentary power of appointment, restricted to the couple's descendants (or descendants and their spouses).

Chapter 13
Drafting for Descendants

For the most part, drafting for descendants means drafting trusts. Only a small percentage of my clients leave their estates outright to all of their children upon the death of both parents. In all other situations, either a child is too young or too irresponsible to receive the property directly, the parents are concerned about protecting the assets from a child's creditors or spouse, or there is a desire to leave an inheritance that will be tax-exempt at a child's subsequent death. Trusts have the flexibility to deal with descendants of different ages, needs, and circumstances.

The Single-Fund Trust

Most couples want to treat their children equally. They believe that to accomplish this they should, after both of them have died, split the trust property into separate, equal trusts, one for each child. However, unless the children are all adults, I usually discuss with my clients the alternative of using a *single-fund trust*.

Typically, the trustee of the single-fund trust is given the discretion to make payments of income or principal among one or more of the descendants, as their respective needs indicate. Should one of the children become ill, require special education, or deserve a particular opportunity (*e.g.*, summer basketball camp, or Northwestern instead of a state university), the trustee can make disproportionate payments among them.

Once the youngest child attains a pre-determined age, the single-fund trust splits into separate, equal trusts for each child. I usually recommend using the age of 22, which is the age by which most children have had the opportunity to complete their college education. The termination of a single-fund trust can also be tied to a specific event, such as college graduation (but with an upper age limit if college is not attended or if one of the children turns into a professional student).

The beauty of the single-fund trust is that it operates just as the parents would have if they had still been living. For example, your daughter qualifies for a select summer music camp. As you are writing out the check, you don't call your attorney to change your estate plan so that her future inheritance is reduced.

Another advantage of the single-fund trust is that it deals with the possibility that both spouses may die, for example, after one child has completed college and another hasn't even started. Without a single-fund trust, the younger child winds up paying for college out of his own one-half share, while Sis got a free ride from her parents.

Some people object to having the older children wait for the youngest to grow up before they get their inheritance. One response to this is to point out that they would have had to wait if the parents were still living—why should an untimely death interfere with the proper care of all of the children? The second response is to make my clients understand that the trustee can always make distributions or loans to the older children to assist them, for example, with the purchase of a home or to start a business, if the trustee is convinced that there are sufficient funds for the younger children. Such distributions can, if desired, be charged as an *advancement* against that child's eventual share.

In most states, children have no absolute right to any portion of their parents' estates. Although the vast majority of people want to treat their children equally, and it has certainly been my experience that children expect to be treated equally regardless of their relative economic situations, there can be valid reasons to do otherwise. For example, I have seen instances where a child has made significant sacrifices to care for a parent, only to find out upon the parent's death that a disinterested sibling receives an equal share because the parent felt obligated to equally divide the estate. In some situations, the children have vastly different earning power, through no fault of their own. While I hate to see people use the threat of disinheritance to force attention or subservience, it can be correct in certain unusual circumstances to treat your children disproportionately.

Children's Trusts

Once separate trusts have been established for the children, the trustee needs to be instructed as to when the children may withdraw the trust property (if at all). Even though the youngest child has attained age 22, or whatever age has been chosen to terminate the single-fund trust, that child, and perhaps others, may still be too young to receive their inheritance outright.

I am a firm believer in allowing only a partial withdrawal in the first instance—what I call the "two bites of the apple" theory. For example, assume each child is given the right to withdraw one third of his or her trust at age 25 and the balance at 30. Even if a child wastes the first withdrawn amount, he or she will have a second opportunity five years later, now older and wiser. Keep in mind that throughout this period of time the trustee will typically have the discretion to make income and principal distributions as the child's needs require.

There is no magic to the ages in my example, though they are usually my recommendation for discussion purposes and many people seem to agree they are appropriate. I have had clients tell me that they want their children to be able to withdraw their entire trusts at age 18, while one of my clients provided that his children could withdraw half at age 60 and the balance at age 70. (He was 75, and felt that he had only recently matured enough to handle his own money!) In larger estates, three bites of the apple are frequently granted, often at ages 25, 30, and 35.

In the meantime, the trustee can be instructed to pay the child either all the income or just so much of the income as the child needs. The trustee should also be given the discretion to make principal distributions to the child. The child's descendants can be designated as additional recipients of discretionary distributions of income and/or principal.

If it is desired that the children receive a required annual distribution, it is often preferable to have the children receive a percentage of the trust value each year, rather than a mandatory payout of the trust income. This prevents the age-old struggle between trustee and beneficiary, where the beneficiary pushes the trustee to invest in high-yielding income securities when, in the long run, that beneficiary would be better off with a portfolio largely consisting of lower-yielding growth securities.

Trusts for Life

Many people prefer that their children will, at some age, be allowed full access to their trusts. However, a good case can be made for keeping part or all of a child's inheritance in trust for the child's lifetime:

- A lifetime trust can protect children with no financial acumen or self-control.

- Properly drafted, a trust protects its assets from the claims of the beneficiary's creditors. If your child is in a high risk profession, a trust can provide him or her with significant peace of mind. The trust language providing such protection is called a *spendthrift clause*.

- In most states, inherited property is exempt from division during a divorce. There is no better way to prove that property is inherited than if it is still in trust.

- Where a child is developmentally disabled, a properly drafted lifetime *supplemental needs trust* can provide an important protection for the child, preventing the trust property from being used up for the child's support where governmental programs would otherwise provide.

- Most importantly, if the child has or will likely have a sizeable estate of his or her own, a lifetime *generation-skipping* trust can provide a significant tax savings by sheltering the trust property from estate taxes at the child's death.

The topic of lifetime trusts is more thoroughly covered in Chapter 14. I urge you to read this chapter thoroughly so that you fully understand that there is an alternative to leaving children their inheritances outright.

Per Stirpes

This is as good a place as any to introduce the term *per stirpes*. This Latin phrase—meaning "by the roots"—is estate planning shorthand for a dispositive plan that would otherwise require a lengthy explanation.

When property is left to a person's descendants *per stirpes*, it means that the property is divided equally among the person's children, but if one of the children predeceases that person, the share that would otherwise have passed to the child instead passes equally among the deceased child's children. If one of that child's children predeceases, the share that would have otherwise passed to that grandchild instead passes equally among the grandchild's children. And so on.

For example, assume Henry and Helen's two children, Tom and Sally, each has children—Tom has two, Sally has three. If, when Helen dies, she leaves her estate to her surviving descendants *per stirpes*, the estate would be split equally between Tom and Sally. Now assume that Tom predeceases his mother. His children will receive the share he would have received, so Helen's estate will be distributed one half to Sally and one quarter to each of Tom's children. Had it been Sally instead of Tom who predeceased Helen, Tom would receive one half and Sally's children would each receive one sixth.

Assume further that not only Sally but one of her children predecease Helen, but that grandchild has two children. Now Tom would receive one half, Sally's two surviving children one sixth each, and Sally's two grandchildren one twelfth each. Finally, assume that neither Tom nor Sally survives Helen, but all five grandchildren do. In most states, including Illinois, Tom's children would each receive one quarter, while Sally's children would each receive one sixth. In some states, however, each of the five grand-children would receive one fifth.

The diagram on the following page may provide a clearer explanation of how a *per stirpital* distribution works. It can be summarized in words as follows:

- Because child 4 is deceased and had no children, there are only three surviving lines of descendants. Each line will receive a one-third share.

- Because child 1 and child 2 are living, they each take a one-third share. Whether or not they have living descendants is irrelevant.

- Because child 3 is deceased but has surviving descendants, those descendants share the other one-third share. Had both of child 3's children been living they each would have received a one-sixth share. Because the deceased child of child 3 has children, those children step up and split that child's one-sixth share.

You should now understand why using the term *per stirpes* is a handy method of shortening an estate planning document!

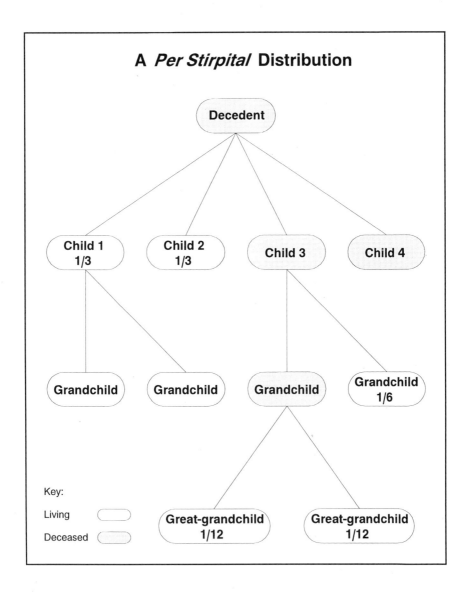

A *Per Stirpital* Distribution

Decedent

Child 1 1/3 Child 2 1/3 Child 3 Child 4

Grandchild Grandchild Grandchild Grandchild 1/6

Key:
Living
Deceased

Great-grandchild 1/12 Great-grandchild 1/12

Trusts for Grandchildren or Other Beneficiaries

When a grandchild, great-grandchild, nephew, niece, or other person becomes a beneficiary, by a per stirpital distribution or otherwise, the instrument should make provision for a trust for each such beneficiary if they are too young to inherit directly. I usually recommend that a trust be created for any beneficiary under the age of 25, to be held until he or she reaches that age. For smaller estates, I recommend the use of the age of 21, so that the trustee can either hold the trust or utilize a custodian account under a Uniform Transfers to Minors Act. For larger estates, I recommend a trust with withdrawal rights at two or three ages, just as is often provided for the children.

Withholding of Distributions

Even when distributions are delayed until a beneficiary attains a specified age, most of my clients seem to like a provision I insert that grants to the trustee the right to withhold distributions if it is determined that, because of the beneficiary's mental state, spending habits, trouble with creditors, or impending divorce, the beneficiary is not able to appropriately deal with the amount distributed. Some clients, however, feel this gives too much power to the trustee and prefer to rely on the pre-determined ages as assuring the competence to deal with the bequests. I always provide that no right of withdrawal can be exercised involuntarily, which provides some protection against creditors or divorcing spouses.

Chapter 14
Generation-Skipping Trusts

The use of generation-skipping trusts is an often misunderstood and underutilized estate planning technique. Mention lifetime trusts for their descendants to most clients and there is an instant negative reaction. There is a belief that trusts are expensive, overly restrictive and give rise to the specter of "hand from the grave" control.

The truth is that a generation-skipping trust can provide a descendant with essentially full access to the funds, yet also provide shelter from death taxes, creditors, and divorcing spouses. Few techniques are so beneficial, yet have almost no downside.

What Is a Generation-Skipping Trust?

A generation-skipping trust is a trust created for the lifetime of a descendant, typically beginning with the children. Because of the manner in which it is established, a generation-skipping trust passes to the next generation free of transfer taxes:

- A generation-skipping trust is not considered to be part of the beneficiary's estate for federal estate tax purposes.

- Just as importantly, a properly established generation-skipping trust is not subject to the federal generation-skipping tax, which is imposed upon the transfer of a decedent's property to grandchildren or other beneficiaries two generations or more removed from the decedent. The generation-skipping tax is imposed at a flat rate of 55%.

The generation-skipping trust is very similar to the estate tax shelter trust that provides such significant tax savings in the estate plan of a married couple. In addition, Illinois has recently joined a few other states in passing legislation so that it is now possible to create a generation-skipping trust that will pass tax free from generation to generation in perpetuity. (Note that it is not the property that skips a generation, just the tax.)

Features of a Generation-Skipping Trust

Trusts are often deliberately restrictive. Where a child is likely to be wasteful, or lacks the ability to manage money, such a trust is often necessary. But what about the child whom the parent wants to be the outright recipient of the parent's estate? Won't a lifetime trust overly restrict the child's use of his or her inheritance? To answer this question, it is important to examine what rights a child can have over a generation-skipping trust without causing the trust to be included in the child's estate for estate tax purposes:

- The child can be the sole trustee of the trust.

- As trustee, the child can have full control over all investment decisions.

- The child can receive all of the trust income.

- As trustee, the child can have the right to distribute to himself or herself so much of the principal of the trust as the child determines to be required for his or her support, health care, and education. The IRS defines "support" as support in accustomed manner of living.

- The child can use the trust property to buy a home or invest in a business.

- As trustee, the child can be given the right to distribute income and principal to his or her spouse and descendants.

- The child can be given a power of appointment over the trust property, which allows the child to determine the ultimate beneficiaries of the trust property. If the child wants his or her children to receive the property outright, instead of in a tax-exempt trust, the child has the power to do this.

Again, please note that these are exactly the same powers a surviving spouse can be granted over the estate tax shelter trust. When you consider all of the foregoing rights, the trust hardly seems unduly restrictive. One way of evaluating the generation-skipping trust is to ask yourself if you would be unhappy inheriting property in such a trust, as long as you had all of the described rights and powers.

Advantages of a Generation-Skipping Trust

Consider the following advantages of a generation-skipping trust:

Creditor Protection

Most states, including Illinois, prevent a creditor from claiming a beneficiary's interest in a trust to satisfy a judgment.

Asset Protection in a Divorce

Under the law of most states, including Illinois, property inherited in trust is not available to a divorcing spouse when the couple's property is divided. When one out of every two marriages ends in divorce, this is an important protection for your descendants.

Economic Support

The trust beneficiary will have an emergency source of support in the event of a financial or medical catastrophe. Because of this, he or she can more readily shift personal assets to younger generation members through direct gifts or trusts, thereby lowering estate taxes on his or her own estate.

Relief From Death Taxes

If a child's personal assets, outside of the trust, are sufficient to create a taxable estate, the inclusion of the trust assets in the child's estate will cause those assets to be taxed at least at 40%, and more probably 50-55%. Assume that a $1,000,000 generation-skipping trust is established for a child, and that the assets of the trust would have been taxed at a rate of 50% if included in the child's taxable estate. Assume further that the child invests the trust assets so that they earn an average annual return of 8%, and that the child annually withdraws 3% of the value of the trust.

In 30 years—the assumed average span between generations—the trust will be worth $4,322,000. The transfer tax savings resulting from having these funds held in a generation-skipping trust for just one generation is $1,161,000. If the child makes no withdrawals, the trust will increase in value to $10,062,000 in the same 30-year period, saving the child's family over $5,000,000 in estate taxes.

These are no small savings. The table on the following page illustrates what would happen to $1,000,000 in two different scenarios: (1) if the amount was not in a trust, and was taxed at each generation, and (2) if it were placed in a perpetual generation-skipping trust (also known as a dynasty trust). The table also shows what happens to the $1,000,000 as the result of 3% average annual inflation. Because of the large amounts involved, the table assumes a 55% death tax rate as each generation dies.

The family whose ancestor has created a generation-skipping trust has created a pool of funds with a buying power over 5½

Skipping Multiple Generations

Year		No GST Plan	GST Plan	3% Inflation
0	Death of creator of generation-skipping trust	$1,000,000	$1,000,000	$1,000,000
30	Death of 1st generation	$4,322,000 -2,377,000 $1,945,000	$4,322,000	$2,427,000
60	Death of 2nd genera-tion	$7,110,000 -3,910,000 $3,200,000	$18,680,000	$5,892,000
90	Death of 3rd generation	$13,830,000 -7,606,000 $6,224,000	$80,734,000	$14,300,000

times the original sum. The family without the benefit of this planning has seen the original pool of funds erode, through estate taxation, to less than half its original buying power.

There is a limit on how many dollars can be allocated to generation-skipping trusts. That limit—called the *generation-skipping tax exemption*—is, as of 1999, $1,010,000 per person creating the trusts, or $2,020,000 per married couple. The number of children is irrelevant. A couple with one child can together create a

$2,020,000 generation-skipping trust for that child; a couple with ten children can create ten $202,000 generation-skipping trusts. Also, be aware that you can establish generation-skipping trusts for some children and not for others.

If the limit is exceeded, the excess funds will be subject to a flat 55% generation-skipping tax at the child's death. Because of this high tax rate and the lack of available deductions, it is recommended that generation-skipping trusts be limited to the exemption amount. The Taxpayer Relief Act of 1997 indexed the exemption for inflation, causing it to increase from $1,000,000 to $1,010,000 effective January 1, 1999. It will further increase annually.

As is evident in the previous examples, once a generation-skipping trust is established within the exemption limits, it can grow without limit and never be again subject to transfer taxes under current law.

Disadvantages of a Generation-Skipping Trust

There are two possible disadvantages to a generation-skipping trust:

- Maintaining a trust means that an income tax return will need to be prepared and filed for the trust each year. However, the fact that the trust is a separate taxpayer provides some tax savings opportunities.

- While the beneficiary/trustee has essentially full control over the trust, withdrawals must be based on a standard related to support, health care, and education, as previously noted. If the trustee makes distributions for non-support items (*e.g.*, round-the-world cruises, expensive jewelry, and furs, etc.), the trustee could be sued for breach of trust by the trust remaindermen, *i.e.*, the beneficiary's descendants. While such suits are unlikely, they do occur.

Conclusion

Many of today's wealthiest families—the Kennedys, DuPonts, Rockefellers, etc.—have maintained their wealth through generation-skipping trusts. People of more modest means often say that such techniques can only be used by the superwealthy. Perhaps it is this thinking that causes such people to have only modest means, while the well-advised wealthy families preserve their wealth. The generation-skipping trust technique is a viable and appropriate technique for any family where future generations are likely to have taxable estates.

Chapter 15
Drafting Other Provisions

Although I am not going to discuss all of the possible provisions of an estate plan, there are a few more that I want to bring to your attention.

Personal and Household Effects

There is a category of assets that typically are disposed of as specific bequests. These assets are personal and household effects—also known as *tangible personal property*—such as clothing, jewelry, china, silver, crystal, art work, electronic devices, furniture, and furnishings. There is an income tax advantage in disposing of these items in a separate provision, but it also makes sense to handle them separately because many people want to dispose of them differently than the rest of the estate.

Generally, most people want their tangible personal property to go to the surviving spouse or, if there is no surviving spouse, in equal shares to their children. Frequently, however, there are certain items that are to pass to certain family members, and these dispositions need to be spelled out. For example, in my practice I have encountered numerous women who want their jewelry to go directly to their children, bypassing their husbands, because they do not want the next wife wearing their jewelry. I have also noticed that many women want their jewelry to pass to their daughters, not their sons, because of their fear that their present or future daughters-in-law will end up with their son's share following a divorce.

One of the advantages of using a living trust instead of a will is that it allows people to change the disposition of personal and household effects by a simple written memorandum. Some states have passed laws permitting this to be done even where a will is the primary estate planning instrument, but in many other states—including Illinois—such a change would have to be executed with the same formalities as the execution of a will. Any do-it-yourself memorandum should be reviewed by counsel, to ensure it does not contain conflicting or ambiguous language.

Specific Bequests

As noted in the first chapter, I generally do not recommend using a *specific bequest* of dollars or property, but strongly recommend using shares or percentages. The primary reason for this is that changing economic circumstances can wreak havoc with even the best-planned estate, causing a specific bequest to become a much larger share of the estate than intended.

However, where cash bequests are quite small in relation to the total size of the estate, I firmly advocate describing them as a specific dollar amount instead of as a percentage distribution. The reason for this apparent flip-flop is that a residuary legatee—one whose share will be affected by the expenses and activities of the personal representative—is in a position to approve or disapprove of the conduct of the administration. Giving a favorite nephew one percent of an estate makes him privy to all of the information about the estate and may require his approval with respect to a variety of administrative matters. If he receives a specific dollar amount, this situation is avoided.

As cash amounts increase in value, there should be an inclination to change them into a percentage or share, or at least put a cap on the bequest, so that it doesn't adversely affect the residuary beneficiaries, who are the primary objects of the decedent's bounty. For example, "I give $50,000 to my nephew, William Olsen, not to exceed 10% of the residuary trust estate, and I give the balance of the residuary trust estate *per stirpes* to my descendants who survive me."

The "Bomb Clause"

I always believe it is appropriate to include a provision for the disposition of the estate in the event everyone in the family dies, especially when children are still living at home or if the family travels together. Such a clause deals with the possibility that parents and children die in a common disaster, or even the possibility that the parents would die, then all of the children would die with no surviving descendants before having withdrawn their trusts. The *bomb clause*, as I call this provision, becomes effective only if there is no surviving descendant of any degree.

Without a bomb clause, the law of intestate succession, discussed in Chapter 3, will control the ultimate disposition of the property. When spouses die in a common accident, this creates the possibility that all or most of the couple's property will pass to the family of the surviving spouse, even if that spouse's survival is only momentary.

For married couples, I usually recommend that each provides in his or her plan that half the property passes to the family or designated beneficiaries of one spouse, while half passes to the family or designated beneficiaries of the other spouse. An exception to this is when one spouse has inherited large amounts from his or her family and feels it is appropriate to pass this wealth back to that family should his or her spouse and descendants all die.

I have drafted bomb clauses ranging from simple bequests to siblings and/or charities to elaborate multi-generational trusts. When the parents of either spouse are still living, I believe it is appropriate to make provision for them in the bomb clause. If this would add to or create a taxable estate, a simple trust can be established that will prevent the taxation of the trust assets in the parents' estates, permitting the assets to pass on their deaths to their other children. Typically, when siblings are named, outright bequests are used.

When nephews and nieces are named, either as contingent or direct beneficiaries, there are usually trust provisions as discussed in the preceding chapter.

I am surprised at the number of people who seem to have no real desire to see their families benefit from their untimely demise, yet are reluctant to make charitable gifts. Ninety percent of my clients name their families as beneficiaries in the bomb clause, sometimes reluctantly. This can be an opportunity to establish a meaningful gift to charity, even though the chances of it ever being made are slim. The famed Newberry Library in Chicago was established as the result of a bomb clause provision in the will of Walter Newberry, that came into effect not from a common disaster, but from all of his children dying without issue.

The *In Terrorem* Clause

An *in terrorem* clause is a useful provision when substantially disinheriting a family member. Such a clause provides that any family member contesting the estate plan loses whatever he or she would have otherwise received.

The *in terrorem* provision is often misunderstood. If a person is being completely disinherited, the clause is of no use because the person has nothing to lose by contesting the plan. Also, the provision is not an absolute bar, for if the person contesting the plan succeeds, the clause is negated.

However, the *in terrorem* clause can be very effective in situations where the non-favored family member is receiving at least a portion of what he or she would normally have received. Because the person is receiving something, the fear of losing that amount usually prevents the person from risking a contest. Not all states give effect to an *in terrorem* clause, but most do, including Illinois.

While on the subject of disinheritance, let me clear up a common misconception. Many people believe that it is better to leave a person one dollar than nothing at all. The one dollar ploy is counter-productive, for it makes such persons beneficiaries. This means they have an involvement in the administration of the estate or trust that could otherwise have been avoided, possibly allowing them to throw a monkey wrench into the works.

It is, however, a good idea to mention a disinherited person in the estate plan so that it is clear that he or she was not omitted through oversight or forgetfulness. A provision such as "I have intentionally omitted my daughter Mary Smith as a legatee and beneficiary under this document" is sufficient. However, giving a reason for the disinheritance is counter-productive—if the beneficiary can convince a judge or jury that the reason is not true, he or she may be able to receive a share of the estate.

Chapter 16
Selection of Fiduciaries

In selecting the *fiduciaries* who will act with respect to your estate, you need to understand the roles each will fulfill. The selection process is extremely important and should be thoroughly discussed with your estate planning advisor.

Trustee

The *trustee*, whether appointed under your trust agreement or pursuant to your will, will have as primary responsibilities the long-term management of the trust investments and the making of discretionary distributions of income and principal to your beneficiaries. In addition, if there is no probate proceeding, the successor trustee under your living trust will be responsible for winding up your affairs, taking possession of your property, discharging your debts, preparing your final income tax returns and preparing the federal estate tax return.

Executor

Your *executor*, who is appointed in your will, should have nothing at all to do if your living trust is fully funded, thus making probating your estate unnecessary. If probate is necessary, your executor will need to work with counsel to accomplish this, after which he or she will then turn the net probate assets over to the trustee. In this case, it is the executor, instead of the trustee, who will exercise most of the "winding up" duties listed in the preceding paragraph.

Guardian

A *guardian of the person* is needed for your minor children. This is the person who will have parental authority over those children. Typically, the children will also reside with this person, although this is not required. A *guardian of the estate* is needed if it is necessary to manage a child's solely-owned assets. If proper planning is done, the only situation in which the child would have such assets is if he or she is entitled to a recovery under a wrongful death action. Guardians are appointed in your will.

Selection of Successor Trustees

I consider the successor trustee of the living trust to be the most important fiduciary involved in your estate plan. There is no magic formula in deciding who this trustee should be. I can only provide you with the following information and suggestions in helping you make that decision.

- As discussed in Chapter 12, for many people the surviving spouse is the logical first successor trustee. A co-trustee to act with the surviving spouse may be required if the spouse needs assistance with money management or investments, or in order to provide assurance that the trust property will be safeguarded for the descendants, particularly in a second marriage situation.

- When the surviving spouse is the first successor trustee, I usually advocate giving that spouse the right to change the subsequent successor trustees. As with the power of appointment discussed in Chapter 12, this provision allows the surviving spouse to deal with changing circumstances that the deceased spouse could not possibly anticipate.

- Co-trustees are permitted and, in some cases, to be encouraged. Any number of co-trustees can be appointed, but if more than two or three are involved, the administration process becomes too unwieldy. Duties can be divided among the trustees, so that one could, for example, handle the investments while the other decides on discretionary distributions.

- Once both spouses are deceased, there are many possibilities for the choice of a successor trustee. Most people choose one or more family members. Adult children should not be over-looked as trustees for younger children, and adult children should definitely be considered as co-trustees of their own trusts. How else is a child to gain the experience of handling his own money unless allowed to participate in the management of his or her trust?

- I am surprised at how often banks and trust companies are overlooked in favor of marginally competent family members. Yes, banks charge a fee, about one percent of the trust assets annually—more for small trusts, less for large trusts. However, for this fee they make all investment decisions, generate periodic accountings, make discretionary decisions, and prepare the trust tax return—and they do these chores very profession-ally. Banks, or at least their trust departments, never die, and their procedures and deep pockets assure no loss through theft or gross ineptitude. The trust assets managed by a bank are not reachable by the bank's creditors or depositors should the bank fail. A bank should be considered anytime the trust assets will, in the aggregate, exceed $500,000. I often urge clients in doubt about whom to name as trustee to visit with a bank trust department. Many find that this is the right answer for them.

- There should always be a string of successor trustees named, ending with a bank or trust company, or there should be some mechanism in place to select successor trustees. Frequently, that mechanism involves granting to the trust beneficiaries the right to appoint successors, with minor beneficiaries repre-sented in this process by their guardians or parents.

Selection of Executor

Typically, the executors will be the same as the successor trustees. Because the executor's duties may be limited, particularly where the probate estate simply pours over to the living trust, a single executor may suffice even if there are co-trustees. Again, it is important to provide for successor executors.

Selection of Guardian

The appointment of guardians for minor children has promoted more heated discussions among my married clients than almost any other matter. Let me share some thoughts with you that should be considered in making this decision.

- With few exceptions, the guardian of the estate should be the same as the trustee. It is permissible to have co-guardians of the estate. As mentioned earlier in this chapter, it is rare that a guardian of the estate will be required to act.

- Frequently, the guardian of the person is the same person who is selected as successor trustee after the death of both spouses. However, some people prefer to separate the functions of taking care of the children and taking care of the trust property. Another strategy that works well is to appoint, as co-trustees, the guardian of the person and an individual or bank better equipped to deal with the administrative and investment duties.

- Most people select family members as guardians, usually siblings. This choice is sometimes made reluctantly, for lack of a better alternative. Keep in mind that the appointment of family members often results in the uprooting of the children from their schools and neighborhoods. Close friends may be a better choice in some situations. Your friends, who are usually neighbors, often have more similar backgrounds and interests than your siblings. Often they are friends because their children are the same ages as and are friends with your children. Choosing friends as guardians for your children may mean much less disruption in their lives should the unthinkable occur.

- While true with any fiduciary appointment, I especially urge you to check with your chosen guardians to make sure they are willing to take on the responsibility of caring for your children.

- It is normal to think in terms of naming a couple as co-guardians. However, particularly when naming family members, you may want to consider naming only your relative, and not his or her spouse, as guardian. This avoids having your children involved in a tug-of-war upon their divorce.

- I frequently use a provision that gives the trustee the authority to assist the guardian in purchasing a new home or expanding or remodeling an existing home. This provision allows the trust and guardian to co-own the new home, and permits the trust to lend money to the guardian. I believe this is an appropriate power. However, it does leave room for overreaching, particularly if the trustee and guardian are the same. One of the best ways of determining the extent of the powers you should give to your guardian and trustee is to imagine what you would feel to be appropriate if you had to take on this responsibility for someone else's children.

Selection of Agents

The selection of agents and successor agents under your power of attorney for property and your power of attorney for health care is discussed in Chapters 7 and 8.

Chapter 17
Avoiding Taxes Through Gifts

Once the estate tax shelter trust technique explained in Chapter 10 has been implemented, the second best method of saving transfer taxes—and the best method for a single individual—is through the use of various gift-giving techniques.

Using the Annual Exclusion

The concept of the gift tax annual exclusion was discussed in detail in Chapter 9. To briefly review, the exclusion is currently $10,000 and can be used to make annual tax-free gifts up to this amount to as many recipients as desired. People with large estates can employ this exclusion to save significant amounts of federal estate taxes that would otherwise be payable at their deaths.

Consider the case of Helen's friend Maude, a 74-year-old widow with a $10,000,000 estate. Maude has two children and four grandchildren, and during each year for the remainder of her 13-year life expectancy let's assume that she gives away $10,000 to each of her six descendants—a total of $780,000. If she had retained the gifted funds, let's assume that she would have invested them at a net after-tax return of 5% and the funds would have accumulated, unspent, in her estate—to a total of $1,176,000.

This gifting program produces a federal estate tax savings at death of $647,000, with no change in Maude's lifestyle. If we take into account the projected increases in the indexed annual exclusion rate, the savings increase to $740,000. If an older single individual can accomplish this savings within a relatively short life span, imagine what a systematic gift program by a younger, married couple could accomplish. Obviously, the number of potential donees, the number of years such gifts can be made and the expected return on investment can significantly alter the figures shown.

Maude's estate may be large, but $740,000 is still a lot of money. You do not need a $10,000,000 estate to employ this technique effectively. Any estate in excess of the exemption amount will reap significant savings from an annual gift program, for keep in mind that the minimum federal estate tax rate is 37%.

Using the Lifetime Exemption

Although the annual exclusion is the most advantageous gift giving technique, the use of the lifetime exemption—$650,000 as of 1999—should not be overlooked. As noted in Chapter 9, to the extent the exemption is used during lifetime, the exemption available at death is reduced, dollar for dollar. There would seem, therefore, to be no advantage in using the exemption during lifetime. However, while any amount that qualifies for the exemption is mathematically brought back into the estate tax calculation, the post-gift appreciation and income with respect to the gifted property are not.

Assume Maude makes a gift of $650,000 into a trust for her children and grandchildren, a trust that achieves an after-tax rate of return of 5%. After 13 years, the original $650,000 trust will be worth $1,225,000. This means that the $575,000 of earnings and appreciation will not be subject to a 55% tax at Maude's death, saving $316,000. By combining a $650,000 gift and the previously-described $10,000 annual gifts, a total of $1,056,000 of federal estate tax can be saved.

Unlike the $10,000 annual gifts, the $650,000 lifetime exemption places virtually no restrictions on the manner in which the property is given. The full $650,000 can be placed in a trust, the beneficiaries do not need to be given a withdrawal right, and no specific allocation of the property among the beneficiaries needs to be made. The trustee can be given the discretion to spray payments of income and principal among a group of beneficiaries, which can change as marriages occur, additional descendants are born, etc. What is required, as with the $10,000 gifts, is that the donor must be willing to irrevocably part with ownership and control of the gifted funds. The donor may not retain any rights to the money nor act as trustee (except with very limited powers).

Taxable Gifts

It is also possible to save a significant amount of money in a large estate through the making of a taxable gift, *i.e.*, a gift in excess of the lifetime exemption and any applicable annual exclusions. Let's assume that Maude would be willing to allocate $3,000,000 of her estate for this purpose, in addition to the exclusion and exemption gifts discussed earlier in this chapter. What can she accomplish by giving away $3,000,000?

First, we have to compute the gift tax that, when added to the net gift, will result in a total expenditure of $3,000,000. The result is that an actual gift of $2,147,000 is made to the descendants, and a gift tax of $853,000 is paid to Uncle Sam. You may think it is crazy to pay a tax to the government before it is necessary, but consider the final result. The $2,147,000 is invested so that it yields an after-tax return of 5%. Thirteen years later, when Maude dies, the $2,147,000 has grown to $4,048,000. We have removed from the taxable estate $1,901,000 of appreciation as well as the $853,000 in gift tax paid.

Removing $2,754,000 from the taxable estate saves $1,515,000 in estate taxes. The cost to the family has been the loss of the earnings from the gift tax paid 13 years prematurely, which is only $774,000, based on our assumed after-tax return of 5%. The technique increases the family's wealth by $741,000.

Given the current 20+% annual returns being produced by the stock market, a 5% average annual return may be a trifle conservative. Using a different format, the table on the next page shows the combined savings of the same annual gift tax program and the same

A Comprehensive Gift Program

Maude is a 74-year-old widow with a 13-year life expectancy and a $10,000,000 estate. Without any gifting, her estate will be taxed as follows:

Starting point	$10,000,000

Average annual return (8%)	$800,000	
Average annual spending	-300,000	
Average annual growth	$500,000	

Estate value after 13 years of compounded growth	$18,856,000
Less: federal estate tax	-10,109,000
Amount passing to children	$8,747,000

The following illustrates what occurs when Maude makes annual exclusion gifts to six descendants and a one-time gift (inclusive of gift tax paid) of $3,625,000:

Value of $60,000 of annual gifts for 13 years (including expected annual growth)	$1,393,000
Value of net gift of $2,747,000 after 13 years	7,539,000

Value of Maude's estate after 13 years

Value without gifts	$18,856,000	
Less: Annual gift program	-1,393,000	
One-time gift	-7,539,000	
Gift tax and foregone		
appreciation	-2,320,000	
	$7,604,000	
Less: federal estate tax	-3,477,000	4,127,000
Amount passing to children		$13,059,000

Savings to family	$4,312,000

one-time gifts of $650,000 and $3,000,000, with an assumed average investment return of 8%. For purposes of this illustration, I have assumed that Maude will spend $300,000 per year.

The Cost Basis Problem

There is a downside to giving away property that should be considered. When appreciated property is gifted, the donee of the gift assumes the donor's original cost basis for purposes of reporting capital gain for income tax purposes (subject to an adjustment for any gift tax paid). On the other hand, if property is held until death, the beneficiaries are allowed to use the federal estate tax value of the property as its basis. This stepped-up basis at death is usually more advantageous to the recipient.

The cost basis of gifted or inherited property has no impact until the property is sold, and it may never be a factor if the donee holds the property until death and in turn receives a new stepped-up basis. However, the amount of unrealized gain in a person's assets should be considered when planning a gifting program. In general, property that has not significantly appreciated should be gifted instead of highly appreciated property.

Tax Savings Aren't Everything

This chapter has illustrated that the federal estate tax can be significantly reduced by a gift program. Even an annual exclusion gift program in the latter stages of life can have beneficial results. However, there are many individuals who, despite knowing that such gift programs can save significant tax dollars, are unwilling to part with ownership and/or control over funds that they have built up throughout their lifetimes and that provide them with perceived security in their old age. In such cases, I believe it is inappropriate to view tax savings as being more important than the psychological and emotional security of the individual.

Chapter 18
Gift Trusts for Minors

The most effective way to make gifts to a minor beneficiary is through the use of a *§2503(c) trust*, so named because a gift to such a trust qualifies for the $10,000 annual exclusion from the federal gift tax pursuant to §2503(c) of the Internal Revenue Code. The trust is also called a *minor's exclusion trust* or, simply, a *minor's trust*.

Gift Tax Considerations

A gift in trust does not usually qualify for the $10,000 annual gift tax exclusion because it is not a *present interest* in property, *i.e.*, the beneficiary does not have unrestricted access to the trust property. However, there is a special provision under §2503(c) that permits gifts made to certain qualifying trusts to be sheltered by the annual gift tax exclusion. In order for a trust to qualify under §2503(c):

- the beneficiary must be under age 21;

- the trust must be unamendable and irrevocable;

- the grantor of the trust must retain no interest in the gifted property;

- the income and principal of the trust must be used exclusively for the benefit of the beneficiary; and

- when the beneficiary attains age 21 (even though the age of majority in the state in which he or she resides may be lower) the beneficiary must be given the right for a period of at least 30 days to withdraw all of the trust property.

Many people do not like the requirement that the beneficiary can withdraw the entire trust at age 21. I recommend to those persons that they use the trust as a means of funding a college education, with the funding and disbursements timed in such a way that the trust is fully expended or nearly so by the time the beneficiary attains age 21.

Even if significant funds remain in the trust at that time, perhaps because the child did not attend college or attended a less expensive school than anticipated, the beneficiary's opportunity to withdraw the trust property upon turning 21 need only be made available for a 30-day period—or window—when presumably the parents still have sufficient influence over the child to discourage a withdrawal. Once the window is closed, the language of the trust can provide that it continues on either for the beneficiary's lifetime or until older ages of withdrawal.

A person other than the original grantor of the trust may make gifts to the trust that also qualify for the $10,000 annual exclusion, thereby permitting a single trust to receive funds, for example, from both parents and grandparents. However, it may be preferable to establish a separate trust for each such donor, to take advantage of the lower income tax brackets available to each separate trust.

Gift Tax Reporting

So long as aggregate transfers to the §2503(c) trust and directly to the trust beneficiary are limited to $10,000 per year per donor, no gift tax return needs to be filed. The donor's spouse may also make a separate $10,000 transfer to the trust with no reporting requirements. A married individual may contribute up to $20,000 to the trust without adverse gift tax consequences if the donor and the donor's spouse file gift tax returns on which they elect to treat the gift as having been made one-half by each.

As noted, gifts made directly to the trust beneficiary—outside of the trust—will reduce the $10,000 exclusion amount available for gifts to the trust. However, this is not the case to the extent the gifts outside the trust are direct payments of the beneficiary's tuition or medical care costs, for such gifts may be made above and beyond the $10,000 annual exclusion.

Income Taxes

The §2503(c) trust is a separate taxpayer, and will pay tax on any income not distributed during the year. Based on the 1999 tax rates (which are shown in the box on the following page), this means that the first $8,450 of income earned each year is taxed at rates lower than the maximum rate of 39.6%, which saves approximately $960 compared to paying the tax at the top marginal rate. It is this ability to save as much as $960 per trust that encourages the establishment of a separate trust by each family member wishing to make gifts.

To the extent income is distributed from a §2503(c) trust to a child who does not attain age 14 by the end of the year in which the distributions occur, the income tax on those distributions will be equal to the amount of income tax the child's parents would have paid if the income had been included in their taxable income. It is generally recommended that no distributions be made before the year the child attains age 14.

Also note that if the trust income is used to discharge a parent's legal obligation of support for a child, the parent will be taxed directly on that income, even if the child is 14 or more. This means that funds should not be expended on such things as food, clothing, shelter, or public schooling. However, there are court cases that permit the expenditure of funds for private schooling, horseback lessons, music lessons, summer camp expenses, etc., without being

Income Taxation of Estates and Trusts

1999 Rates

Taxable Income	Tax	% of Excess
0	0	15%
$1,750	$262.50	28%
$4,050	$906.50	31%
$6,200	$1,573.00	36%
$8,450	$2,383.00	39.6%

subject to tax, because these items are typically not legal obligations on the part of the parents. The law in this area varies from state to state and is constantly changing, so be careful. There are certain jurisdictions, for example, that have ruled that a parent has a legal obligation to provide a college education to a child if the parent can afford it. Illinois is not yet among them.

Another potential trap is that trust funds should not be used to discharge liabilities on behalf of a child for which the parent has become personally obligated. For example, if the child's school requires the parent to sign a contract guaranteeing the payment of the tuition, or if there is an express or implied agreement between the parent and the school that the parent will be responsible for these payments, the trust's payment of tuition is deemed by the IRS to be for the parent's benefit, not the child's. This will cause the income so expended to be taxed directly to the parent. One way to handle this problem is to have the trust contract for and guarantee any tuition payments, with the school waiving the parent's individual responsibility.

Trustees

It is possible for the trust grantor or the parent of the trust beneficiary to be the trustee of a carefully drafted §2503(c) trust without any adverse income tax consequences. However, if the parent of a trust beneficiary is the trustee (regardless of the identity of the donor) and dies prior to the trust beneficiary attaining age 21, all of the value of the trust will be includible in that parent's estate for federal estate tax purposes. If the trust is small, many consider the inclusion for federal estate tax purposes to be a reasonable trade-off for the parent being able to control the trust property. If the amount is large, however, it is generally advisable to use a non-parent as a trustee.

The Uniform Transfers to Minors Act Account

Every state has a *Uniform Transfers to Minors Act* (or *Uniform Gifts to Minors Act*) that permits the creation of *custodian accounts* with provisions very similar to the §2503(c) trust. Gifts to such accounts also qualify for the annual $10,000 gift tax exclusion. However, a §2503(c) trust is a far more flexible vehicle for making gifts to minors:

- A custodian account must be terminated and distributed to the beneficiary at age 21. As previously noted, a §2503(c) trust need only provide a short window during which the beneficiary may terminate it, after which it can continue indefinitely.

- The income earned by custodian account is taxed to the child whether or not it is actually distributed to the child, and it is taxed at the parents' marginal tax rate if the child is under 14 and if the funds originated from either parent. The income of a §2503(c) trust is taxed to the trust unless distributed.

Chapter 19
Life Insurance

As noted in the introduction, I am not going to discuss in great detail the question of how much insurance you should buy. However, I would like to discuss briefly the need for insurance. I believe insurance is absolutely essential if either of the following is true:

- The insured's family needs the life insurance proceeds to replace the insured's earning power so as to maintain their accustomed manner of living.

- There is a need for liquidity to pay estate taxes so as to avoid the forced sale of assets.

Even if neither of these conditions is present, insurance can still make sense as an investment vehicle. Insurance is a unique asset in that it offers all of the following advantages:

- The accumulation of value inside a life insurance policy is exempt from current income taxes.

- The policy proceeds paid at death are also exempt from income taxes.

- Estate taxes with respect to the policy can be completely avoided with proper planning.

Many people believe that qualified retirement plans and IRAs offer the best possible investment vehicles. Retirement plans are

wonderful at the front end, but at the back end, particularly after
death, the taxation of these plans can be almost confiscatory, as
discussed in Chapter 21. The tax benefits available from life
insurance may be better suited to your needs. I urge you to listen
carefully to your life insurance agent. There can be much more to
life insurance than simply a death benefit—it can also be an
excellent investment vehicle.

Consider the following comparison of life insurance to qualified
retirement plans and IRAs:

Life Insurance	Retirement Plan
Premiums not income tax deductible.	Contributions income tax deductible.
No current income tax on policy earnings.	No current income tax on plan earnings.
Lifetime withdrawals in excess of premiums paid subject to income tax.	Lifetime withdrawals taxable and may be subject to penalty.
Cash value may be borrowed.	Borrowing permitted up to $50,000.
Death benefits not subject to income tax.	Death benefits subject to income tax.
Death benefits subject to estate taxes, but this tax is avoidable.	Death benefits subject to estate taxes.

Beneficiary Designations

Assuming you own some life insurance, how should it be dealt
with from an estate planning point of view? As pointed out in
Chapter 11, insurance is best paid to a living trust. The trust should

be designated as the primary beneficiary, for example: "The acting trustee of the Henry A. Doe Trust dated December 19, 1998."

If no living trust is used, but your will provides for the residue of your estate to be held in trusts established in that will, your insurance should be made payable to your testamentary trustee. Appropriate language for this would be: "The trustee named or to be named in my last will and testament."

If there are no trusts established under your will, it may be better to name your estate as the beneficiary of the insurance than to name individuals, so that your will disposes of the insurance proceeds. The only disadvantage of this is that it will make the insurance proceeds subject to the claims of your creditors, which would not otherwise be the case. Also, in some states—but not Illinois—paying insurance to the estate subjects it to a state inheritance tax that would otherwise be avoided.

Generally the least desirable choice is to designate individuals as beneficiaries, particularly if any of them are minors.

Estate Taxation of Life Insurance

Many people are surprised to learn that life insurance is subject to estate taxes at death. This includes group and individually-owned insurance, term and whole life. The surprise may stem from the fact that they are not used to thinking of their insurance as an asset, or perhaps they remember their insurance agent explaining that life insurance can pass free of estate taxes. This latter statement is true, but only if proper planning is done.

So long as the insured retains any *incidents of ownership*, the life insurance policy is subject to federal estate taxes. Incidents of ownership not only include actual ownership of the policy, but also each of the following:

- the right to the cash value;
- the right to dividends;
- the right to terminate the policy;

- the right to determine ownership; and
- the right to determine the beneficiary.

Retention of any of these rights will cause the insurance to be taxable for estate tax purposes.

One of my clients recently wondered if he could solve the estate tax problem by having his spouse own the insurance policy on his life. This is not an effective technique. If his wife survives him, the insurance proceeds will be taxed at her subsequent death to the extent they are not spent. If his wife does not survive him, the insurance will wind up back in his hands, or at least taxable in his estate, unless very careful planning is done.

My persistent client then suggested that his children could own the policy. This can be an effective technique, for the insurance proceeds will pass to the children upon their father's death with no estate taxes payable, provided he survives the transfer of the insurance to the children for three years. However, this technique does present some possible drawbacks:

- Having the children own a life insurance policy bypasses the surviving spouse, which is usually not desirable for married persons.

- There have been instances of children cancelling the insurance to get at the cash value in the policy.

- Some mechanism should be in place to ensure that the children proportionately contribute the insurance proceeds toward the payment of the estate tax.

Irrevocable Life Insurance Trust

There is a way to have your cake and eat it too. In this context, it is the use of an *irrevocable life insurance trust*, to which the estate planning community has assigned the acronym of ILIT. While the ILIT will be discussed in great detail in the next chapter, for the moment be aware that an ILIT can make provision for the surviving spouse and descendants without causing the insurance proceeds to be taxed for estate tax purposes in either the insured's or the surviving spouse's estate. This technique should be considered by a married couple with combined assets—including insurance—in excess of $1,300,000 and for a single person with more than $650,000.

Second-to-Die Life Insurance

There is an insurance product that closely fits the estate planning needs of many people. The unlimited marital deduction has the effect of delaying any estate taxes until the death of the second spouse. While this is usually well-advised, it does create a significant need for liquidity at the second death, when all of the estate taxes are due.

There is insurance that pays off upon the death of the second to die of two insureds—called, appropriately, *second-to-die life insurance*. It is also sometimes referred to as *survivor (or survivorship) life insurance*. Second-to-die insurance can be significantly cheaper than regular single-life insurance and provides liquidity exactly when it is needed, regardless of which member of the couple predeceases the other. Such insurance is available at reasonable rates even when one member of the couple might be individually uninsurable.

The premium illustrations provided in connection with such insurance should be carefully reviewed, for some products charge significantly higher premiums after one of the insureds is deceased, which may be when the surviving spouse can least afford it.

Second-to-die insurance typically should be owned either by the children or by an ILIT, as there is usually no need for either member of the couple to own such insurance (unless one of the reasons for purchasing the insurance is to permit later access to any cash value build-up).

Accidental Death Insurance

A common trap many people fall into is the purchase of significant amounts of accidental death insurance. Why do they do this? Because accidental death insurance is very cheap. It is cheap because the odds of your dying accidentally are very low.

Why is it a trap? Because your need for insurance does not change depending on the manner in which you die. Whether you die of a heart attack or in a car accident, your spouse and children still need support and your estate still needs liquidity to pay taxes and expenses. You are better advised to take the premium dollars being spent on accidental death insurance and buy more regular life insurance, even if the life insurance purchased is only a fraction of the accidental death insurance you could purchase with the same dollars.

The same reasoning applies to so-called double indemnity insurance—life insurance that pays double if you die in an accident. Again, it is better to purchase more regular insurance.

Chapter 20
The Irrevocable Life Insurance Trust

Buying insurance to meet estate tax obligations can often resemble a dog chasing its tail. An unmarried person with a $5,000,000 estate—the tax on which would be $2,198,000—has to purchase $4,900,000 of life insurance in order to pay the total tax obligation on the resulting $9,900,000 taxable estate. Fifty-five percent of the insurance purchased is required just to pay the additional tax on the insurance!

Insurance need not be taxable in the insured's estate. The best and most frequently used technique to keep insurance from being taxed at death is the *irrevocable life insurance trust*, or ILIT.

Estate Tax Avoidance

An ILIT keeps insurance from being taxed for estate tax purposes because all incidents of ownership are held by the trust —none by the insured. In order to accomplish this the insured must establish an irrevocable trust, irrevocably assign existing insurance to the trust (or have the trust buy a new policy), and irrevocably name the trust as the beneficiary of the insurance. The insured cannot be a beneficiary or a trustee of the trust.

This sounds as though the insured is giving up a great deal. However, in most cases this is not true. Life insurance death benefits, by definition, are unavailable to the insured during lifetime. The purpose of most insurance is to protect the family and provide liquidity for estate taxes. An ILIT fulfills these purposes admirably, for the insurance proceeds are typically held in a trust with exactly the same provisions as the estate tax shelter trust described in Chapter 10. In fact, one way of looking at an ILIT is that it is a way of increasing the size of the estate tax shelter trust by the amount of the insurance proceeds. The following diagram illustrates the use of an ILIT as part of a plan that also includes a marital trust and an estate tax shelter trust.

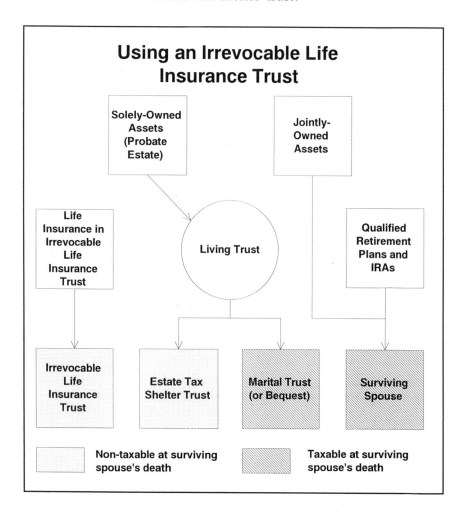

The insurance proceeds cannot be directly available for the payment of estate taxes, but the trustee of the ILIT can lend money to the insured's estate or living trust, or can purchase assets from those entities, thereby providing the necessary liquidity to the entity responsible for paying the estate taxes.

You are probably aware that some kinds of insurance have an investment element, such as cash value, that builds up in the policy and is available to the insured through borrowing or withdrawal. There is no method by which such insurance can be placed in an ILIT and still have the investment element directly available to the insured. However, the trustee can use the investment element to pay premiums, leave it invested in the policy, or make distributions to the trust beneficiaries, who are usually the insured's spouse and descendants. In considering the use of an ILIT with this type of insurance, the insured must choose between the direct availability of the investment element and the estate tax savings available through an ILIT.

The Internal Revenue Code imposes a three-year waiting period before any transfer of insurance is deemed excluded from the insured's estate. There is, however, a relatively simple way around this rule if new insurance is being acquired, which is to first create the ILIT, then have the ILIT apply for the new life insurance. Because the insured never owns the policy, there is no transfer of insurance (just the cash necessary to purchase the insurance), so the three-year waiting period is inapplicable. Obviously, if there is existing insurance that cannot be replaced, this option is not available, in which case the three-year waiting period will apply. Group insurance is one example of insurance that is often assigned to such trusts but cannot avoid the three-year rule.

An ILIT can produce significant estate tax savings. Keeping insurance out of the taxable estate can save between 37% and 60% of its face value.

Gift Tax Avoidance

Since an ILIT is irrevocable, any additions to it can result in taxable gifts. The cash value of any existing insurance policies transferred to the trust upon its creation, as well as all insurance premium payments, are examples of such additions. In order to qualify these additions for the $10,000 annual gift tax exclusion, it is necessary for the creator of the trust to grant to one or more individuals the right to withdraw from the trust an amount equal to any such additions. This withdrawal right is known as a *Crummey power*, named after the legal case that first permitted its use.

The IRS requires that those persons granted Crummey powers of withdrawal also be beneficiaries of the trust. This typically means that only the insured's spouse and descendants can have a right of withdrawal. It is also necessary that proper procedures be observed with respect to such withdrawal rights. The trustee must give the power holders written notice at least annually explaining their rights of withdrawal, and the power holders must be given a fair opportunity to make a permitted withdrawal. Minor children can be represented by a parent, usually the parent who is not the grantor of the ILIT.

It has been my experience that those granted powers of withdrawal do not exercise them, although there can be no binding agreement not to do so. The person making additions to the trust each year can be given the right to designate who will have a withdrawal right with respect to the contributed property. That person can also adjust his revocable estate planning documents to deal with a beneficiary who has exercised a withdrawal right. The knowledge that these two powers exist is generally sufficient to deter any withdrawals.

To the extent a beneficiary is granted a right of withdrawal from an ILIT, the annual $10,000 gift tax exclusion with respect to other gifts made to that beneficiary is reduced, even if no property is withdrawn.

Caution: A bill was introduced in Congress in 1998 to revoke the long-established rule in the Crummey case, which would result in all additions to ILITs being taxable for gift tax purposes, thus gradually using up the donor's transfer tax exemption. The bill did not pass, but there may be some sentiment in Congress for closing this loophole.

Drawbacks to the ILIT

The obvious drawback to an irrevocable life insurance trust is that it is irrevocable. The insured may not retain any right of ownership over the insurance policies, any right to change the beneficial enjoyment of the trust property, or any right to act as trustee. These restrictions can be circumvented in a carefully drafted irrevocable life insurance trust by granting such powers to the insured's spouse. So long as there is a happy marital situation, the granting of such powers to the spouse can be the essential equivalent of having the insured retain those powers. Powers to change the trust provisions (such as a power of appointment) can also be given to others.

Changing family circumstances can be difficult to deal with when an irrevocable insurance trust is in place. An obvious situation is where a child has fallen out of favor and is no longer to be a beneficiary of the couple's estate plan. While it is possible to give to the spouse or another person the right to change beneficiaries, a person other than the spouse will be reluctant to disinherit one of the insured's children. I recommend that people use an irrevocable insurance trust only where there is a stable marital and family situation.

Chapter 21
Naming Retirement Plan Beneficiaries

Individual retirement accounts (IRAs) and *qualified retirement plans* (which I will collectively refer to as retirement plans) are a unique type of property. Retirement plans are wonderful vehicles for building up assets during lifetime. Typically, contributions to a plan are tax deductible for income tax purposes, and earnings within a plan are not currently taxed. However, when the funds are paid out, either during retirement or at death, they are pure taxable income. At death, they are also taxable for estate tax purposes. These two taxes can take away as much as 78% of a plan's value!

The primary purpose of this chapter is to help you designate the beneficiary of your retirement plan so as to minimize your overall tax liability and carry out your estate planning objectives. To do this I need to explain a number of tax concepts that are extremely complicated, even by Internal Revenue Code standards. I will try to make them as easy to understand as possible without omitting essential information. I will then provide an easy-to-follow decision tree at the end of this chapter to assist you in determining the correct beneficiary designation for your situation.

In discussing retirement plans, I will use the term *plan participant* to describe the person who created the IRA or who has an interest in a qualified retirement plan account.

Qualified Retirement Plans versus IRAs

Qualified retirement plans (*e.g.*, profit-sharing, Keogh, 401(k), 403(b), and pension plans) and IRAs are similar in many ways.

However, it would be a mistake to assume that the rules applicable to one group also apply to the other. Qualified retirement plans and IRAs are subject to different Internal Revenue Code provisions. Also, while the rules governing distributions from IRAs are imposed solely by statute, the rules governing distributions from qualified plans are often dictated by the provisions of the plan document.

Some qualified plans have limited distribution options at retirement and at death. Sometimes only *lump-sum distributions* are permitted. If this is the only option available at retirement, the plan participant will usually want to rollover the lump-sum payment to an IRA, which will then be governed by the IRA distribution rules. Alternatively, a qualified plan may permit an annuity payment for the joint lives of the participant and his or her spouse (a *joint and survivor annuity*) or, if the participant is unmarried, an annuity for the participant's life. Even when such distribution options are available, many plan participants will opt for the lump-sum distribution option, if available, with a subsequent rollover to an IRA.

A married participant in a qualified retirement plan is required by statute to name his or her spouse as the beneficiary upon the participant's death, although the spouse may agree to an alternative beneficiary designation by a written, notarized consent. There is no requirement that the spouse be named the beneficiary of an IRA. This means that the protection afforded a spouse by federal law with respect to a qualified plan ends as soon as the participant becomes eligible to take a lump sum distribution and roll it over to an IRA.

The rules discussed in the balance of this chapter apply to IRAs and, unless noted, to qualified plans, except to the extent that the qualified plan provisions provide otherwise.

Distributions Following Retirement

A basic assumption of this chapter is that most people will want to delay distributions from their retirement plans as long as possible. They do this to postpone the payment of income tax and to benefit from the tax-deferred build-up within the plan. Of course, if the funds are needed sooner, or in greater quantities, they can be withdrawn from an IRA in any amount (but not from a qualified plan when an annuity pay-out option has been selected).

Despite this desire to leave funds within a plan, the law requires, at a certain point in time, that the plan participant begin to withdraw a certain amount each year. This amount is called the *required minimum distribution* and the time by which such distributions must start is called the *required beginning date*.

Required Beginning Date

Generally, the required beginning date is April 1 of the year following the year in which the plan participant attains age 70½. For participants in many qualified plans (except for certain owners of 5% or more of the company establishing the plan), this date can be extended until April 1 of the year following the year of retirement.

Required Minimum Distribution

The required minimum distribution for any year is computed by dividing the value of the participant's interest in the retirement plan as of the end of the preceding year by the combined life expectancy of the participant and a *permitted designated beneficiary*. If a permitted designated beneficiary has not been named, only the participant's life expectancy is used.

For example, Sam celebrates his seventieth birthday on June 1, 2000. He will therefore turn 70½ on December 1, 2000, so 2000 is the first year for which he must make a withdrawal. For that first year, he must withdraw the required minimum distribution from his retirement plans by April 1 of the next year, *i.e.*, April 1, 2001. In the future, Sam will have to make his withdrawal by the end of the current calendar year, *e.g.*, his withdrawal for 2001 must be made by December 31, 2001. (Sam may want to make his first withdrawal during 2000 to avoid making two withdrawals in 2001.)

Sam is a widower and names his estate as the beneficiary of his retirement plans. Because an estate is not a permitted designated beneficiary, Sam may only use his own life expectancy in determining the required minimum distribution. For the year Sam attains age 70½, that life expectancy is computed from the IRS tables based on the age of 70.

At age 70 Sam has a life expectancy of 16.0 years, and his first withdrawal—for the year 2000—must be 1/16 of his interest in his retirement plan valued as of the end of 1999. For 2001, when his life expectancy is 15.3 years, he must withdraw 1/15.3 of his interest valued as of the end of 2000, and so forth. The table on the following page shows the life expectancies used to compute the required minimum distributions based on a single life.

Sam does not have to withdraw all of the money in 16 years because he is allowed to recalculate his life expectancy each year. In the previous example, even though Sam became one year older when he went from 70 to 71, his life expectancy only decreased 0.7 years. This method of computing the minimum required distribution—the *recalculation method*—is one of two methods allowed by the IRS, but is the method that truly results in the minimum possible distribution. Using this method assures Sam of having a life expectancy until he reaches 115, when his life expectancy finally becomes zero in the table.

Alternatively, Sam could use the *declining balance method*, which requires that his life expectancy be reduced by one for each year he lives. The use of this method will cause Sam to withdraw his account balances in 16 years (*i.e.*, 1/16 the first year, 1/15 the second, 1/14 the third, and so forth). Once Sam elects a calculation method, the choice is irrevocable. If he selects neither method, the recalculation method is deemed to have been elected.

The penalty for failing to make the required minimum distribution is an excise tax equal to 50% of the difference between the required amount and the amount actually withdrawn. Note: there is no required minimum distribution for a Roth IRA during the plan participant's lifetime.

Life Expectancies Used to Compute Required Minimum Distributions Based on a Single Life			
Age	Life Expectancy	Age	Life Expectancy
70	16.0	86	6.5
71	15.3	87	6.1
72	14.6	88	5.7
73	13.9	89	5.3
74	13.2	90	5.0
75	12.5	91	4.7
76	11.9	92	4.4
77	11.2	93	4.1
78	10.6	94	3.9
79	10.0	95	3.7
80	9.5	96	3.4
81	8.9	97	3.2
82	8.4	98	3.0
83	7.9	99	2.8
84	7.4	100	2.7
85	6.9		

Source: Treas. Reg. §1.72-9, Table V

Permitted Designated Beneficiaries

A beneficiary should be designated for any retirement plan interest. In a perfect world—one without taxes—this would be for the purpose of identifying the recipients of the interest in the plan upon the participant's death and defining the method by which they received this property. However, the identity of the beneficiary affects the computation of the minimum required distribution during the plan participant's lifetime and beyond, and it determines the taxation of the plan interest for both income and estate tax purposes after the participant's death. Let's first look at the impact of the beneficiary designation on the required distributions.

As previously noted, the minimum required distribution amount can be computed using the joint lives of the plan participant and the beneficiary, if the beneficiary is a *permitted designated beneficiary*. A permitted designated beneficiary means:

- any individual; or

- a trust, so long as (1) it becomes irrevocable on the participant's death, (2) it has identifiable individual beneficiaries, and (3) either a copy of the trust agreement or a detailed summary of the trust provisions is lodged with the administrator of the qualified plan or the financial institution managing the IRA prior to the participant attaining age 70½. It is believed (perhaps "hoped" is a better word) by the estate planning community that the third requirement will be eliminated or substantially changed in the near future.

Prior to 1998 it was also necessary that the trust be irrevocable during the participant's lifetime, but the IRS then ruled that a typical living trust can be a permitted designated beneficiary. This is another advantage of a living trust, for a person's probate estate cannot be a permitted designated beneficiary, and it is still unclear whether or not a testamentary trust can be.

When a permitted designated beneficiary is used, the computation of the minimum required distribution is based on both the participant's age and the age of the permitted designated beneficiary, using the table set forth on the following page. In calculating the age of the beneficiary, there are a number of concepts which you need to understand:

Partial Table of Life Expectancies Based on Two Lives

Age of Plan Participant

		70	71	72	73	74	75	76	77	78	79	80	81	82
	60	26.2	26.0	25.8	25.6	25.5	25.3	25.2	25.1	25.0	24.9	24.8	24.7	24.6
	61	25.6	25.3	25.1	24.9	24.7	24.6	24.4	24.3	24.2	24.1	24.0	23.9	23.8
	62	24.9	24.7	24.4	24.2	24.0	23.8	23.7	23.6	23.4	23.3	23.2	23.1	23.0
A	63	24.3	24.0	23.8	23.5	23.3	23.1	23.0	22.8	22.7	22.6	22.4	22.3	22.3
g	64	23.7	23.4	23.1	22.9	22.7	22.4	22.3	22.1	21.9	21.8	21.7	21.6	21.5
e	65	23.1	22.8	22.5	22.2	22.0	21.8	21.6	21.4	21.2	21.1	21.0	20.8	20.7
	66	22.5	22.2	21.9	21.6	21.4	21.1	20.9	20.7	20.5	20.4	20.2	20.1	20.0
o	67	22.0	21.7	21.3	21.0	20.8	20.5	20.3	20.1	19.9	19.7	19.5	19.4	19.3
f	68	21.5	21.2	20.8	20.5	20.2	19.9	19.7	19.4	19.2	19.0	18.9	18.7	18.6
	69	21.1	20.7	20.3	20.0	19.6	19.3	19.1	18.8	18.6	18.4	18.2	18.1	17.9
B	70	20.6	20.2	19.8	19.4	19.1	18.8	18.5	18.3	18.0	17.8	17.6	17.4	17.3
e	71	20.2	19.8	19.4	19.0	18.6	18.3	18.0	17.7	17.5	17.2	17.0	16.8	16.6
n	72	19.8	19.4	18.9	18.5	18.2	17.8	17.5	17.2	16.9	16.7	16.4	16.2	16.0
e	73	19.4	19.0	18.5	18.1	17.7	17.3	17.0	16.7	16.4	16.1	15.9	15.7	15.5
f	74	19.1	18.6	18.2	17.7	17.3	16.9	16.5	16.2	15.9	15.6	15.4	15.1	14.9
i	75	18.8	18.3	17.8	17.3	16.9	16.5	16.1	15.8	15.4	15.1	14.9	14.6	14.4
c	76	18.5	18.0	17.5	17.0	16.5	16.1	15.7	15.4	15.0	14.7	14.4	14.1	13.9
i	77	18.3	17.7	17.2	16.7	16.2	15.8	15.4	15.0	14.6	14.3	14.0	13.7	13.4
a	78	18.0	17.5	16.9	16.4	15.9	15.4	15.0	14.6	14.2	13.9	13.5	13.2	13.0
r	79	17.8	17.2	16.7	16.1	15.6	15.1	14.7	14.3	13.9	13.5	13.2	12.8	12.5
y	80	17.6	17.0	16.4	15.9	15.4	14.9	14.4	14.0	13.5	13.2	12.8	12.5	12.2
	81	17.4	16.8	16.2	15.7	15.1	14.6	14.1	13.7	13.2	12.8	12.5	12.1	11.8
	82	17.3	16.6	16.0	15.5	14.9	14.4	13.9	13.4	13.0	12.5	12.2	11.8	11.5
	83	17.1	16.5	15.9	15.3	14.7	14.2	13.7	13.2	12.7	12.3	11.9	11.5	11.1
	84	17.0	16.3	15.7	15.1	14.5	14.0	13.5	13.0	12.5	12.0	11.6	11.2	10.9

Source: Treas. Reg. §1.72-9, Table VI

Note: The shaded boxes represent the maximum number of years a designated beneficiary other than a spouse may be younger than the plan participant.

- When a trust is a beneficiary, the age of the oldest trust beneficiary is used.

- Similarly, when multiple beneficiaries are named, the age of the oldest beneficiary is used.

- If the beneficiary is other than the spouse, that beneficiary can be considered to be no more than ten years younger than the plan participant. These are the ages highlighted in gray in the table on the preceding page.

- The actual age of the participant's spouse can be used regardless of the age differential.

- The beneficiary's age can be recalculated each year, but only if that beneficiary is the spouse. This is called the *dual recalculation method*.

Because Sam wants to take distributions from his retirement plan as slowly as possible, he is counseled upon approaching his required beginning date to name his children as the beneficiaries of his retirement plan. His oldest child is 45, but Sam may not use an age younger than 60 in computing his required minimum distribution. Therefore, Sam must withdraw 1/26.2 of his interest in the plan for the year he turns age 70½. Sam can achieve the same rate of distribution by naming his living trust as beneficiary, so long as his children are its beneficiaries and a copy of the trust is provided to the plan administrator or custodian.

It is extremely important to understand that it is the beneficiary designation and life expectancy calculation method in place on the participant's required beginning date which irrevocably controls the rate at which the plan must be withdrawn, both during the participant's lifetime and, for many situations, following the participant's death. The beneficiary designation can be changed, but the withdrawal rate can never be less than that permitted by this prior designation. No matter what designation was recommended to you when you were younger, you should consult with your advisor well in advance of your required beginning date to determine the most effective beneficiary designation to use at that time.

Distributions at Death

The rules governing distribution at death are particularly complex. First, let's consider the rules that are applicable if the participant dies before reaching the required beginning date. If this occurs, the general rule is that the proceeds must be withdrawn by the end of the year during which the fifth anniversary of the participant's death occurs, subject, however, to two extremely broad exceptions:

- If the beneficiary is the surviving spouse, he or she has two additional options:

  o The surviving spouse may rollover the plan proceeds to his or her own IRA (or create a new IRA for that purpose). The spouse is free to designate a new beneficiary and use that beneficiary's life expectancy in computing the minimum required distribution upon reaching the required beginning date.

  o The surviving spouse also has the option of treating the participant's IRA as an *inherited IRA* upon the participant's death. This prevents the spouse from designating a new beneficiary to extend the payout, but it does allow the spouse to delay distributions until the year after the year in which the participant would have attained age 70½. This is beneficial for a spouse who is considerably older than the participant. Also, if the surviving spouse is under the age of 59½ and later realizes he or she needs access to the funds while still under that age, there will be no early distribution penalty.

- If the beneficiary is not the spouse, but is a permitted designated beneficiary, the beneficiary may withdraw the retirement plan over his, her, or its (in the case of a trust) life expectancy, using the declining balance method. That first beneficiary's life expectancy irrevocably locks in the minimum rate at which the plan proceeds must be paid out, even if the beneficiary dies prior to full distribution of the plan.

If the participant has reached the required beginning date, then the beneficiary designation in effect as of that date and the method of calculating life expectancies selected by the participant greatly influence how the retirement plan interest is distributed on the plan participant's death:

- If there was not a permitted designated beneficiary in place on the required beginning date, the entire account balance must be distributed before the end of the year following the year of death if the participant dies after the required beginning date. This rule alone is reason enough to carefully review the beneficiary designations on all retirement plans upon attaining age 70½.

- If there was a permitted designated beneficiary on the required beginning date, and that beneficiary is still living at the participant's death, the interest in the plan may be paid out over that beneficiary's lifetime. If the participant's life expectancy was being calculated using the declining balance method, the participant's remaining life expectancy can also be used (even though the participant is deceased). If the recalculation method was being used, the participant's life expectancy is recalculated to zero at death, and only the beneficiary's life expectancy can be used.

- If the permitted designated beneficiary dies before the participant, the results can be especially harsh. As previously mentioned, a new beneficiary can be designated, but the original beneficiary's life expectancy must be used in determining the payout during the participant's remaining lifetime and after the participant's death. If the beneficiary's life expectancy was being recalculated, the beneficiary's death reduces that life expectancy to zero, which means that only the participant's life expectancy can be used. If the dual recalculation method was being used, both life expectancies are reduced to zero, which means that the plan proceeds must be fully paid out by the end of the year following the year of the participant's death, even if the participant designated a new beneficiary. For this reason, it is generally recommended that the recalculation method be used for the participant's life and the declining balance method for the beneficiary's life.

- If the beneficiary is the surviving spouse, that spouse has the right to make a *spousal rollover*, just as was the case if the participant had not reached the required beginning date.

The Spousal Rollover

There is one key exception to the general rule that retirement plan benefits are taxable at (or beginning with) the participant's death. As noted in the preceding section, the surviving spouse—and only the surviving spouse—has the right to rollover the lump sum proceeds of a retirement plan to his or her own IRA, thus avoiding any income tax at this time. Also, because the spouse is the beneficiary, there is no estate tax with respect to the plan proceeds because the proceeds qualify for the estate tax marital deduction. Thus the spouse may continue to invest the funds without paying current income taxes and may defer distributions from the rollover IRA until he or she is past the age of $70\frac{1}{2}$. There are two other reasons the use of a spousal rollover is advantageous:

- The surviving spouse need not begin to receive distributions from his or her own IRA until attaining age $70\frac{1}{2}$, which means that a surviving spouse younger than the deceased participant can benefit from additional income tax deferral.

• The surviving spouse may use a new beneficiary designation, creating additional income tax deferral based on the age of the oldest beneficiary, adjusted for the ten-year maximum age differential.

The spousal rollover achieves tax deferral, not tax avoidance. Eventually, someone will pay income taxes on the plan proceeds. However, the ability of the surviving spouse to achieve this tax deferral is usually so advantageous that I almost always recommend that the spouse be named as the primary beneficiary, even if the estate tax shelter trust winds up being underfunded as a result.

The one drawback to a spousal rollover is that it prevents penalty-free access by the surviving spouse to the plan proceeds until he or she attains age 59½, although a partial rollover can be used to free a portion of the funds for immediate use.

It is also possible to use the spouse's age in determining the minimum required distribution, yet retain control over the ultimate distribution of the retirement plan proceeds. This can be accomplished by naming the marital trust created under the participant's living trust as the primary beneficiary. The drawback to this technique is that such a trust does not have the ability to make a tax-deferred rollover and must therefore pay income tax upon the distribution. Deciding between a tax-deferred rollover and retaining control over the ultimate distribution of the problem is a particularly sticky problem, particularly in second marriage situations where interests in retirement plans are a major portion of the estate.

The Roth IRA

The new *Roth IRA*, which was introduced by the Taxpayer Relief Act of 1997, is a somewhat different savings vehicle and requires a separate explanation.

- Unlike a conventional IRA, there is no income tax deduction allowed for contributions to a Roth IRA. (A Roth IRA can be funded either by annual contributions or by converting a conventional IRA to a Roth IRA, although funding by conversion creates a current income tax liability.)

- Like a conventional IRA, earnings within a Roth IRA are tax-deferred.

- Unlike a conventional IRA, distributions are non-taxable.

- Otherwise, all of the IRA rules and regulations apply to the Roth IRA.

Even though the distributions from a Roth IRA are non-taxable, I still recommend that the spouse be the primary beneficiary of a Roth IRA so that the spouse may rollover the plan to her own IRA and continue to enjoy the tax-free buildup within the plan. As with the conventional IRA, the younger the spouse, the more beneficial the rollover. Also, I generally recommend that the participant's living trust be named as the secondary beneficiary.

Keep in mind that if the participant's estate tax shelter trust will be underfunded, the Roth IRA is the first choice from among the participant's retirement plans to be payable to the participant's living trust so that it can be allocated to the shelter trust.

Determining the Beneficiary Designation

As I warned you, the foregoing discussion was full of complexity. The following is an attempt to simplify the decision-making process. To determine the correct beneficiary designation for your situation, you need to answer three questions, then use the decision tree on page 138 to determine the correct primary beneficiary of your retirement plans. The questions are:

Married?

This one is easy.

Need to Shelter?

For those married persons who do not have sufficient other assets to fully fund the estate tax shelter trust, the only funds available for this purpose may be from the retirement plans. As I have suggested in Chapter 11, it is often better to forgo the estate tax savings in favor of the spousal rollover. However, when the estate savings are deemed more important, a beneficiary designation that permits the retirement plan proceeds to pass into an estate tax shelter trust is desirable. As previously mentioned, a Roth IRA should be the first choice to be used to fund a shelter trust.

Control?

Do you believe it is important to control the administration and ultimate distribution of the retirement plan proceeds? Such control could be important in any situation where you question the beneficiary's ability to handle the plan proceeds or are concerned about whom the beneficiary will name as the ultimate beneficiary. Where control is desired, be sure to work closely with your estate planning advisor.

In using the decision tree on the following page, you will see how your answers will lead you to one of four beneficiary designations:

Surviving Spouse

For most married individuals, the beneficiary of choice will be the surviving spouse. This will be the result whenever the retirement plan assets are not deemed necessary to fund the estate tax shelter trust and when the plan participant is willing to have his or her

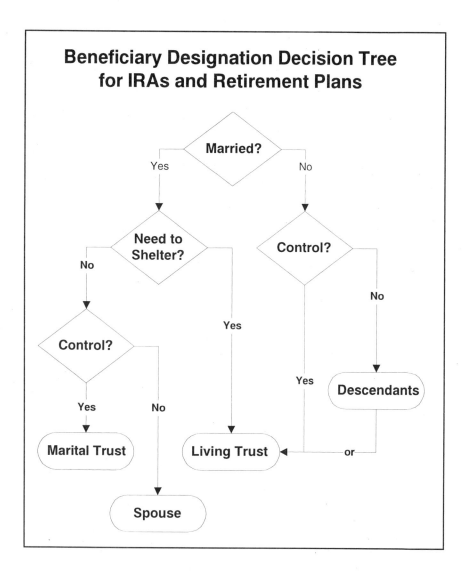

spouse control the plan proceeds. In fact, even if it is deemed desirable to shelter the retirement plan assets from estate taxes, the plan proceeds can be left to the surviving spouse, who can then disclaim a sufficient amount to fund the shelter trust. Whenever the surviving spouse is the primary beneficiary, the living trust should usually be the secondary beneficiary.

Marital Trust

Whenever:

- the participant is married,

- it is not necessary or desired that the plan proceeds be estate tax sheltered, and

- control over the post-death plan proceeds is desired,

the proceeds should be payable to the marital trust created by the living trust. This trust presumably sets up the desired control over the trust property. It is very important to work with your estate planning advisor in drafting the beneficiary designation in this situation. Again, the living trust should usually be the secondary beneficiary.

Descendants

There is one set of circumstances where a plan participant may want to name his or her descendants as beneficiaries. This would be when an unmarried participant is fully comfortable with the idea of his or her children receiving the plan proceeds outright. This avoids the need to file a copy of the living trust or a list of the beneficiaries with the plan administrator. The participant might consider creating multiple IRAs, with each designating a different child as the beneficiary. This permits each child, upon ultimately inheriting the IRA, to choose the rate at which they take distributions and to tailor the investment portfolio to his or her particular needs.

Even though the participant feels comfortable with an outright distribution, the beneficiary designation may not deal with what happens if a child predeceases, nor include any of the other provisions that have been carefully drafted into the living trust. Therefore, paying the proceeds to the living trust is often preferred.

Living Trust

The living trust will usually be the primary beneficiary of choice for an unmarried participant. No secondary beneficiary needs to be named.

The use of the foregoing decision tree does not depend on whether or not the participant has reached the required beginning date. To repeat once more, however, it is important to thoroughly review your beneficiary designations upon approaching age 70½, as well as to decide which recalculation method you will use.

The rules governing the distributions from retirement plans are unnecessarily complex. Even worse, they often prevent the participant from following a rule I have tried to stress in this book—using a single document to govern the disposition of all of your assets. The designation of the beneficiary of your retirement plans is one area where you will want to work very closely with your estate planning advisor.

Chapter 22
Gifts and Bequests to Charities

The federal estate tax permits an unlimited charitable deduction for gifts at death to qualified charitable organizations. This means that anyone who is determined not to pay any estate tax upon death merely has to bequeath any excess over the exemption amount to charity. For every dollar given to charities at death, somewhere between 37¢ and 60¢ is saved in taxes.

However, don't become overly enamored with the tax benefits of outright charitable gifts at death. Another way to look at it is that for every dollar given directly to charities at death, between 40¢ and 63¢ is taken away from your non-charitable beneficiaries.

Lifetime Charitable Gifts

For those who can afford it, lifetime charitable gifts are much more effective than gifts at death. The reason is that a lifetime gift not only removes the gifted amount from the estate, but also provides a current charitable income tax deduction.

Helen Doe wishes to assist her alma mater, and believes she can spare $100,000 from her estate during her lifetime. Her $100,000 gift creates a $100,000 income tax deduction, which permits Helen (over the course of a few years) to save $28,000 in income taxes (based on an assumed marginal income tax rate of 28%). At death, her estate, now depleted by $72,000, saves an additional $31,000 in estate taxes, for a total savings of $59,000. It has only cost the family $41,000 to make a $100,000 charitable gift—Uncle Sam picked up the balance. In the highest tax brackets, the net cost to the family would only be $27,000.

There is a limitation on the amount of charitable contributions that can be deducted for income tax purposes in any one year. For gifts to public charities no more than 50% of the donor's *contribution base* (*i.e.*, adjusted taxable income without regard to any net operating loss carryback) can be deducted. There is a five-year carryover available for unused deductions.

Split-Interest Gifts

There are several methods of giving a gift to both charitable and individual beneficiaries that fall under the category of *charitable split-interest gifts*. Let's first examine such a gift where the donor is also the individual beneficiary. Assume that our rich widow Maude from Chapter 17 puts $2,000,000 into a either a *charitable gift annuity*, a *pooled income fund*, or a *charitable remainder trust*. In each case, Maude receives either the income or a fixed payout from the $2,000,000 during her lifetime, but upon her death the remaining funds pass to charity. Even though Maude has parted with none of the income from her investments, she achieves a current charitable income tax deduction based on the present value of the future charitable gift. If Maude is 74 when she establishes the gift, and receives an annual payout of 7%, the present income tax deduction would be approximately $1,000,000, with the exact amount depending on the type of technique used and the then current interest rate used by the IRS in making this calculation.

Assuming Maude is in the top income tax bracket, her charitable gift saves her about $400,000 during her lifetime, with no loss of income. To look at it another way, in return for Maude's pledging a $2,000,000 gift to charity at death and agreeing not to touch the principal of the gift during her lifetime, Uncle Sam agrees to put $400,000 in Maude's pocket.

It is sometimes possible to take the income tax saving derived from a charitable remainder trust and use it to purchase an insurance policy that has a face value greater than the amount given to charity. Now the family is ahead of the game by utilizing this technique, with the only disadvantage being the loss of access to the trust principal. Such insurance is best owned by an irrevocable life insurance trust. The coupling of a charitable remainder trust and an irrevocable life insurance trust is often referred to as either a *make-up trust* or a *wealth replacement trust*.

Maude can also save estate taxes upon her death by establishing—either during her lifetime or at death—a split-interest gift whereby a beneficiary receives a payout for a term of years or life, with the remainder to charity. This technique is used most often with siblings, parents, or childless children.

For example, Maude places $1,000,000 at her death into a charitable remainder trust that is to pay out 7% of its initial value each year to a sister ten years younger, after whose death the trust distributes to charity. Based on the government tables, the sister's interest is deemed to be worth $436,000 and the charitable remainder interest is worth $564,000. The charitable deduction saves $310,000 in estate taxes.

In a variation on this theme, a *charitable lead trust* can be used, by which a fixed payout is made to charity for a term of years, after which the trust is distributed to descendants. This can be particularly attractive if the investment yields will greatly exceed the projections.

To illustrate, assume that Maude places $1,000,000 into a charitable lead trust at her death that is to pay out 7% of its value each year to a charity for 15 years, after which the trust will distribute to her descendants. Based on current government tables, the charitable interest is deemed to be worth $647,000, while the remainder interest is worth only $353,000. The charitable deduction saves the family $356,000 in estate taxes. Assume that the fund is invested aggressively in common stocks, with the investment advisor able to achieve an average annual after-tax return of 10%. At the end of the fifteen-year term, the trust will have increased in value to $1,558,000, even though it pays out 7% of its value to charity every year.

Now let's assume that no charitable gift is made and the children invest the after-tax amount of $450,000 in the same way. At the end of 15 years the children would have $1,880,000. The present value of the $322,000 differential is only $80,000. This $80,000 figure is the cost to the family of making a charitable gift of $647,000—Uncle Sam pays the other $567,000.

This chapter has covered only the basic charitable giving techniques. Those with charitable inclinations should work with the planned giving office of their favorite charity and/or their estate planning attorney to understand the full scope of the charitable gifting arrangements that are possible.

Chapter 23
Protecting Assets From Creditors

Many people believe trust lawyers have a magic solution that will enable them to protect their assets from the claims of current or anticipated creditors. Unfortunately, there are no fool proof strategies that accomplish this goal. The discussion in this chapter will, if nothing else, alert you to the cardinal rule of asset protection, *i.e.*, plan before there is a problem.

Transfers in Trust

Persons wishing to protect assets from creditors often ask if they can place their assets in a trust and retain the use of those assets by naming themselves as beneficiaries. While it is true that trusts can be used to protect assets from creditors, Illinois does not permit a person to create a creditor-protected trust for his or her own benefit. When a person creates a trust and retains an interest in that trust—even though the trust is irrevocable and contains a spendthrift clause—the trust property is subject to claims.

A person can create a trust for another, even a family member, that is protected from the beneficiary's creditors. Such a trust would contain a *spendthrift clause* (*i.e.*, a creditor protection clause). Such a trust must be irrevocable. And, so long as the grantor retains no interest in the trust, the trust property will also be protected from the grantor's creditors, unless the transfer is deemed to be a fraudulent conveyance. This will be discussed in more detail in the next section.

Protection of Assets Through Transfers

The only truly effective method of protecting assets is the irrevocable transfer of those assets to another—in trust or outright—with no strings attached. There are, however, significant legal restrictions on such transfers of which you should be aware.

Fraudulent Conveyances

If a creditor or a trustee in bankruptcy can show that a transfer is a *fraudulent conveyance*, the transfer can be nullified. The Illinois statutes define a fraudulent conveyance as any transfer made:

- while the transferor is insolvent or that causes insolvency (defined as either balance sheet insolvency or the inability to pay debts as they become due); and

- with intent to hinder, delay, or defraud creditors (present and future); and

- for inadequate consideration.

The intent requirement is not necessary if (1) the transfer was voluntary, (2) there was insufficient consideration, (3) there was an existing or contemplated specific indebtedness (as opposed to a merely possible future indebtedness), and (4) the debtor retained insufficient assets to discharge the indebtedness. Intent is implied in such a situation.

There is a five-year statute of limitations from the date of a fraudulent conveyance during which a creditor can bring an action under the Illinois statute to set aside that transfer. A trustee in bankruptcy under the federal bankruptcy law also has the same rights as creditors under state law, thus giving the trustee a five-year period during which such transfers can be recovered.

Although transfers for insufficient consideration between spouses are not presumed to be fraudulent, the courts have ruled that such a transfer by an insolvent spouse will be very closely scrutinized.

What all of this means is that it is very difficult to make transfers that are creditor-proof at a time when a person is either insolvent or is threatened with insolvency. However, a transfer made at a time when the transferor was clearly solvent has an excellent chance of withstanding creditor attack.

Estate Planning Considerations

Not only should transfers be made prior to insolvency or threatened insolvency, the impression that such transfers are designed to hinder creditors should be carefully avoided. One of the best methods of accomplishing this is to make transfers that further estate planning goals.

As discussed in Chapter 10, transfers from the wealthier spouse to the less wealthy spouse are recommended so that, no matter which spouse dies first, there are sufficient assets to fund an estate tax shelter trust at that death. Frequently the result of this planning is to cause the couple's home, investments, and cash to be titled in the name of the non-working spouse, who is less likely to have creditor difficulties. These assets are exactly the ones that will most benefit from being protected from the wealthier spouse's creditors.

Divorce Considerations

No transfer between spouses should be contemplated without the possibility of divorce being considered. As discussed in Chapter 11, transfers to a spouse may result in the transferred assets being deemed the separate property of the transferee spouse. A postnuptial agreement can address this issue, if desired.

Offshore Trusts

A detailed discussion of offshore trusts as a means of protecting assets from creditors is beyond the scope of this book. It should be noted that persons who are seriously concerned about claims against their property may find that an offshore trust can provide the necessary protection. However, establishment of an offshore trust involves certain disadvantages, such as lawyers' and trustees' fees, loss of ready access to the trust funds, loss of the ability to use offshore assets in obtaining credit, and a certain element of risk in placing assets in a foreign jurisdiction. In considering this step, be sure to consult an attorney who specializes in this area.

Other Thoughts on Transferring Assets

As previously noted, transfers designed to frustrate creditors can be made in trust. It is possible that the donor spouse can be a trustee of the trust, but for a variety of estate tax, income tax, and creditor protection reasons, the powers of that trustee must be carefully circumscribed. It is usually preferable that the donor spouse not be a trustee.

Transfers can be made to anyone, not just to spouses. However, as previously noted, the transfers must be complete, with no retained rights in the donor. While a donee spouse will presumably use the transferred property for the couple's living expenses, there is no such assurance with respect to gifts to others.

Reciprocal gifts should be avoided. For example, the technique of two siblings setting up trusts for each other or each other's family is not effective.

There are certain types of interests that cannot or need not be transferred. Interests in professional corporations cannot be transferred to non-professionals and the transfer of interests in other entities may be restricted by agreement. Life insurance proceeds are immune from creditors, as is the current value of life insurance policies, except as to premiums paid in fraud on creditors. Qualified retirement plans and IRAs cannot be transferred, but are generally protected from attachment by creditors.

Summary

Anyone concerned about possible future creditors should take steps to protect his or her property by irrevocable transfers well before problems arise. Transfers to a spouse may also be beneficial from an estate planning point of view, and concerns about a future divorce can be solved by a postnuptial agreement. The tax, property law, divorce law, and estate planning considerations involved in such transfers should be reviewed with a lawyer to be sure the transfers are made in the most advantageous way.

Chapter 24
Planning for Medicaid Qualification

Qualification for Medicaid is a topic of great interest to many families. It is also an area about which there is a great deal of confusion. This chapter provides detailed guidelines as to what can and cannot be done in order to qualify for Medicaid.

What is Medicaid?

Medicaid is a government program designed to help the neediest of individuals pay for long term institutional health care. Medicaid is not part of Medicare. It is a program administered by the states that is partially funded by the federal government. Subject to the federal statutes dealing with this program, each state sets its own guidelines as to qualification for Medicaid. There is, however, a great deal of similarity among the states as to these guidelines.

Who Qualifies for Medicaid?

In Illinois, a person qualifies for Medicaid if his or her circumstances meet the following criteria:

- The person must be over 65, blind, or disabled.

- The person's income must be less than the cost of the nursing home. If the person is married, income is determined by the name on the check or underlying asset. If the check or asset is in both names, each is deemed to receive one half. Income is determined after subtracting a $30 per month personal needs allowance, an allowance for a dependent spouse or child, medical bills not paid by Medicaid, and medical insurance premiums. The remaining income must be used to defray the nursing home expenses; Medicaid pays the balance.

- The assets of the person are immaterial to whether or not the person qualifies for Medicaid. However, assets in excess of permitted amounts must be spent before Medicaid will begin paying for nursing home expenses.

What Assets Can a Qualifying Person Retain?

The process of obtaining funding from Medicaid requires spending down or giving away assets until a person is essentially impoverished. In Illinois, only the following assets are exempt:

- The person's residence, but only if a spouse, sibling, or minor or disabled child resides there, or if the person reasonably expects to return to the residence. In addition, if the person is likely to return home within six months, a home maintenance allowance may be retained.

- Cash or other assets of not more than $2,000. Cash includes money in joint accounts, unless it can be proven that the person's interest in or access to the account is less than the whole.

- Personal effects of a reasonable value (generally not more than $2,000).

- Wedding and engagement rings, and items needed by reason of the person's medical condition, regardless of value.

- A motor vehicle required for employment, essential daily activities, and/or transportation for medical treatment.

- A pre-paid burial plan or life insurance policy up to $1,500.

- Burial plot, casket, mausoleum space, or similar asset.

Assets in excess of the foregoing must be spent for nursing home care before Medicaid will provide funds.

Assets of the Spouse

In the case of a married person, the non-institutionalized spouse may retain or be given what is known as the community spouse asset allowance, which is adjusted annually for inflation and is currently about $80,000. Under the federal rules the assets of both spouses are considered as a single fund, so that the community spouse asset allowance is the limit that can be held by the non-institutionalized spouse. However, the Illinois rules permit the non-institutionalized spouse to hold his or her individually-owned property, even if that property has a value in excess of the community spouse asset allowance, so long as no additional transfers are made to that spouse. Such individually-owned property must not have been transferred within the preceding 36 months.

Post-Death Claims

The foregoing exemptions and allowances are only applicable during lifetime. In Illinois, state statute reserves for the Illinois Department of Public Aid the right to make a claim against the estate of a person who has received benefits and also against the estate of that person's spouse. Therefore, even if a couple has protected their home, an expensive wedding ring, an automobile, or other assets, these assets cannot be freely bequeathed to the couple's children or other beneficiaries (with the exception of minor or disabled children).

Transfers of Assets to Avoid Medicaid Rules

Many people want to know how the foregoing rules can be avoided by gifts or transfers to trusts. They want to retain access to their assets while still qualifying for Medicaid assistance. However, the Medicaid rules regarding transfers make this extremely difficult.

People assume that if they give away their assets to their children, they will then be able to qualify for Medicaid. However, the Medicaid rules provide that any transfers made within the past 36 months are counted when determining what funds Medicaid will provide. For example, assume a person has given away $100,000 during the past 36 months in order to reduce assets to the required levels. The Illinois Department of Public Assistance, which administers the Medicaid program, will either (1) require that $100,000 of nursing home expenses be paid by that person before making any Medicaid funds available, or (2) consider the person ineligible for the time required to expend $100,000 on nursing home care.

People next ask if they can establish a trust that will accomplish the desired goal, *i.e.*, a so-called Medicaid Qualifying Trust. However, the Medicaid rules are even stricter with respect to transfers into trust, for they require that all such transfers made within the last 60 months be counted in determining a person's assets. Also, if such trust has any discretionary provisions that can be exercised in favor of the nursing home resident, Medicaid rules require that the maximum amount that can be distributed to that person must be used for nursing home expenses before Medicaid will cover any costs, whether or not the distributions are actually made. These rules also apply to trusts established by a spouse.

The foregoing rules do not apply to discretionary trusts established by someone other than the person or the person's spouse. Such trusts are sometimes referred to as "supplemental needs" trusts and they are exempt for Medicaid purposes if carefully drafted.

However, if the funds used to create the supplemental needs trust originated from the person for whom the trust is being created, the law requires that the transactions be collapsed and treated as if the person had created a trust for himself.

One exception to the transfer rules is that a residence may be transferred to a child under the age of 21, a disabled or blind child, or a child who has provided care to the parent and who has been residing in the parent's residence for two years prior to the date the parent enters the nursing home.

Recommendations

The most effective way to qualify for full Medicaid assistance is to give away all assets except those needed for living expenses for a 36-month period, then wait 36 months before applying for Medicaid assistance. Private nursing home insurance can be purchased to cover the gap period. Other strategies might be to pay off any mortgage on the house or improve the house, if it is exempt; to buy a more expensive engagement and/or wedding ring; and to prepay funeral and burial expenses.

There is also a quality of life issue that needs to be carefully considered. Although most nursing homes participate in the Medicaid program, those familiar with nursing homes will acknowledge that there is often a significant difference in the physical surroundings and quality of care given to Medicaid patients versus private pay patients. Many nursing facilities have the same room type available for both types of patients, but place three to a room on the Medicaid floors versus one or two to a room on the private pay floors. There may also be a difference in the staff-patient ratio.

While no one wants to pay the high cost of nursing home care if they think they can get the government to do it for them, the quality of life may not be nearly as pleasant in a Medicaid environment. Those who can afford the private pay rate should consider carefully before entering into a long-term plan to impoverish themselves in order to qualify for governmental assistance.

Chapter 25
Henry and Helen Revisited

This is a good opportunity to rewind and revise history for Henry and Helen. You may recall that our couple from the first chapter owned in joint tenancy a $300,000 residence, a $300,000 brokerage account, and $400,000 of bank accounts. In addition, Henry had a $200,000 insurance policy on his life.

The hero of this retelling of the story will be an attorney. However, it might have been an accountant, insurance agent, trust officer, or financial planner—anyone who could have counseled Henry and Helen on the appropriate ownership and disposition of their assets. Only the attorney of this group, however, can draft the necessary legal documents to implement the plan.

One day Henry's boss Frank told Henry about an estate planning attorney with whom he and his wife had met the previous day. Frank was quite enthusiastic about what he had learned, for he believed the advice he had been given would save his family a great deal of money. He urged Henry to make sure his own estate plan was in order, if he had not done so already. Somewhat reluctantly, Henry called the attorney and made an appointment for Helen and himself.

After learning about Henry and Helen's assets, the attorney explained to them the advantages of living trusts and the estate tax shelter trust technique. He urged them to split ownership of their assets, retitling them into their respective trusts. When he showed them how the suggested plan would save their children anywhere from $82,000 to $216,000 or more in estate taxes, depending on how long they lived, and would also avoid probate and ensure an equal distribution of their property between Tom and Sally, Henry and Helen decided to proceed.

The attorney drafted living trusts, pourover wills, and powers of attorney for property and health care for both Henry and Helen. Once the documents had been reviewed and discussed, they were signed. The attorney then prepared deeds by which the couple's home would be transferred into Helen's trust, and provided the couple with a letter explaining how to allocate and retitle their assets.

Henry was advised to transfer the $300,000 stock portfolio into his name, as there were a number of greatly appreciated securities in the account. Because Henry was the more likely to die first, his ownership of the stocks would provide a stepped-up basis for the property. Henry was also advised to name his trust as the beneficiary of his $200,000 life insurance policy and to transfer a $100,000 bank account to his trust. Henry now had $600,000 with which to fund a shelter trust if he died first.

Besides the $300,000 home, Helen's trust was to own the remaining $300,000 in bank accounts, which meant that her trust would also own $600,000 which could be used to fund a shelter trust if she were the first to die. It took some prodding from the attorney, but the couple finally retitled all the accounts as suggested. They now owned all their property in one of their two trusts, or had designated their trusts as beneficiary.

When Henry died in 1999, Helen was concerned about her access to the money in Henry's trust. She visited the attorney, who assured her that, as the sole trustee, she had essentially full access to the trust property. She asked if he would explain in detail what would happen to Henry's property.

The attorney first told her that because Henry's trust was smaller than the allowable $650,000 exemption, all of his property would become part of the estate tax shelter trust created upon his death. There would be no marital trust.

From the shelter trust, Helen could pay herself income or principal for her support in her accustomed manner of living and for health care. She even had the power to make distributions to her children or grandchildren if she desired, but the decision was solely hers. Helen had full control and authority over the shelter trust.

At Helen's subsequent death all of the property in the estate tax shelter trust would pass tax-free to Tom and Sally, even if the trust had grown in value in the meantime. Because of this, the attorney advised Helen that even though she had access to the shelter trust, she should avoid using it for her expenses as much as possible. She should instead utilize her own assets, even if it meant dipping into her principal. In this way, the shelter trust would be free to grow in value, protecting her in the event her personal funds ever ran out and providing tax shelter for the children.

Once Helen understood and felt comfortable that the assets of the shelter trust would always be available to her, Helen followed the attorney's advice for the most part. She left the brokerage account, alone, reinvesting all dividends and interest. She did take the income from the $300,000 of cash in the shelter trust, which was now invested in a bond fund. Helen found that she was able to live quite comfortably on the income from this fund and her own $300,000 in cash, once her banker worked with her to maximize the interest rates on her cash investments.

Except for withdrawing some of the income, there was not much Helen needed to do to administer the shelter trust. Her accountant prepared an income tax return for the trust every year, and her broker provided her with monthly statements, from which she was pleased to learn of the significant increase in value during the years following Henry's death.

When Helen became ill and was no longer able to manage her financial affairs, Sally exercised the power in the trust documents to become the successor trustee of both her mother's trust and her father's estate tax shelter trust, with the approval of Helen's personal physician. She used the power of attorney for property to transfer one small account that was still in Helen's name into her trust, but otherwise Sally was able to manage all of her mother's affairs through her role as successor trustee of both trusts. As trustee, she was able to sell the house without any difficulty, investing the proceeds as part of her mother's trust.

When she found the job of trustee becoming somewhat time-consuming, she and her brother agreed that she should take a modest fee for her services, as she was permitted to do pursuant to the document. Tom was relieved that he did not have to try to deal with his mother's financial affairs from a half-continent away.

When Helen passed away, her personal estate was a little less than $700,000, which was the threshold amount for filing a federal estate tax return in 2003. With no estate tax return to file, and no probate proceeding, Sally learned from her mother's lawyer that as soon as she had paid her mother's outstanding bills, which only involved the nursing home and a few doctors bills, she was free to distribute her mother's trust and the $800,000 currently in the shelter trust. Within several months after her mother died, Sally had completed all of the necessary administrative steps and had distributed property valued at $1,500,000 in equal shares to herself and her brother.

This is quite a contrast from the unhappy result of Henry and Helen's planning as set forth in Chapter 1. It only required a little planning, some retitling of assets, and a relatively modest legal fee.

Glossary

accidental death insurance — insurance that pays only if the insured dies because of an accident, rather than an illness.

advance health care directive — a term that describes any document by which a person can indicate in advance what type of health care treatment he or she should receive under specified circumstances. In Illinois, this term refers to the living will and the power of attorney for health care. In other states, this term may encompass surrogate health care forms and advance medical directives.

advancement — a lifetime gift or post-death bequest or distribution that is charged against the recipient's share of the donor's residuary estate.

affidavit of domicile — a document certifying the state of domicile of the owner of a security. A necessary document for the transfer of any security.

agent — a fiduciary office created under a power of attorney. An agent is given the authority to act for another person (the principal) under certain specified circumstances.

ancillary probate — a probate proceeding in a state or country other than the decedent's state of domicile, usually required when the decedent owns real property in that other jurisdiction.

annuity — an arrangement whereby a periodic payment of (usually) a fixed amount is paid to the annuitant, typically for life.

ascertainable standard — a guideline to a trustee in the making of discretionary distributions that is limited to support, health, and education. An ascertainable standard must be used when the beneficiary is the trustee and it is desired to exclude the trust from the trustee/beneficiary's estate for death tax purposes.

assignment separate from certificate — also known as a stock power (or bond power), this instrument is used to transfer ownership of a security.

attorney in fact — an agent under a power of attorney.

beneficial interest — generally, an interest enjoyed by a beneficiary in any trust. In Illinois, this also refers to a beneficiary's interest in a land title trust.

beneficiary — a person or entity that is entitled to the benefits of a trust, usually the right to receive payments of income and principal.

beneficiary designation — a written direction designating the recipient of property such as insurance or retirement plans following the death of the insured or participant.

bomb clause — a provision in a will or trust establishing the ultimate distribution of property in the event the person, the person's spouse, and all of the person's descendants should die before all of the property is distributed.

bond power — an instrument used to transfer ownership of a bond, more formally known as an assignment separate from certificate.

charitable remainder trust (CRT) — a trust that provides an annual payment to one or more individuals, typically for life, with the subsequent remainder interest payable to charity, resulting in a current charitable income tax deduction to the creator of the trust.

charitable lead trust (CLT) — a trust that provides an annual payment to charity for a term of years, followed by a distribution to individual beneficiaries, resulting in a current charitable income tax deduction to the creator of the trust.

charitable split-interest gift — any continuing trust that has both charitable and non-charitable beneficiaries. Unless such a trust is carefully drawn, meeting very specific statutory rules, the charitable portion of the gift will not qualify for a charitable deduction. Examples of charitable split-interest gifts are the charitable remainder trust, charitable lead trust, pooled income fund, and charitable gift annuity.

charitable gift annuity — similar to a charitable remainder trust, in a charitable gift annuity the donor makes an irrevocable gift to a charity, and the charity agrees to pay the donor (and/or one or more specified beneficiaries) an annual annuity for life or specified time period, upon the completion of which the charity keeps any remaining funds. The donor achieves a charitable income tax deduction at the time of the gift.

community property — in nine states, a form of ownership by a married couple in which earnings during marriage, and property acquired with those earnings, are deemed to be owned equally by the spouses.

conservator — in Illinois, a term formerly used for the guardian of an incompetent adult.

contribution base — adjusted taxable income without regard to any net operating loss carryback. Used in connection with determining the maximum amount of charitable donations that can be deducted for income tax purposes in any one year.

cost basis — typically, the value at which an asset is acquired, used in determining capital gain or loss upon the subsequent disposition of the asset. Upon death, an asset's cost basis is stepped-up to its federal estate tax value.

Crummey power — a limited right of withdrawal given to a trust beneficiary that allows additions to a trust to qualify for the annual gift tax exclusion.

custodian — the name of the fiduciary office established under any Uniform Transfers (or Gifts) to Minors Act.

death tax — the all-encompassing term for the taxes charged upon a person's death, including both estate and inheritance taxes.

declining balance method — a simplified method of computing the required minimum distribution from a retirement plan that does not permit the participant's life expectancy to be recomputed each year.

deed in trust — a deed used to convey real property into a trust. Different than a trustee's deed, which is used to convey real property out of a trust.

designated beneficiary — in general usage, any beneficiary designated by the owner of a life insurance policy, IRA, qualified plan, or other asset permitting the use of a beneficiary. The Internal Revenue Service uses the term to mean a beneficiary of an IRA or qualified retirement plan whose relationship to the plan participant is such that the beneficiary's life span can be used in computing minimum payouts from the plan. In this book, such a beneficiary is described as a *permitted designated beneficiary* to avoid confusion.

disclaimer — the refusal to accept a gift or inheritance, often a useful tool for saving estate taxes.

dual recalculation method — a method of computing the required minimum distribution from a retirement plan which takes into account the life expectancy of both the plan participant and a beneficiary.

durable power of attorney — a power of attorney that is effective even if the principal (*i.e.*, the creator of the power) becomes incompetent.

dynasty trust — a multi-generational trust that is exempt from all transfer taxes as each generation dies—a method of keeping family wealth intact.

estate planning — the process of passing accumulated wealth to a person's beneficiaries, upon death or during lifetime, in trust or outright, with a minimum of transfer taxes and administration expenses.

estate tax — a tax imposed at death upon the value of a decedent's estate.

exclusion — for estate tax purposes, property qualifying for an exclusion is not included in the gross estate for transfer tax purposes. There is a fine, but meaningful, distinction between an exclusion and an exemption.

executor — the person charged with the responsibility under a will of administering the decedent's probate estate. This is a short-term responsibility that ends once the estate is distributed to its beneficiaries or into trust. With proper planning, the nominated executor will have no job, for all of the decedent's property will pass under his or her living trust.

exemption — property qualifying for an exemption is included in the gross estate for transfer tax purposes, but is exempt from that tax. Because of the marginal rate structure, the inclusion of exempt property in the gross estate uses up the lower tax brackets and causes additional, non-exempt property to be taxed at higher rates.

federal estate tax — the estate tax imposed by the federal government on the estates of all citizens and residents of the United States, as well as the United States property of non-resident aliens.

fiduciary — derived from the Latin for "faithful," a blanket term describing several offices that may be created as part of an estate plan, such as executor, trustee, guardian, agent, and custodian.

fraudulent conveyance — the legal phrase used to describe a transfer that illegally defeats the interest of creditors, usually because it is made at a time when the transferor is insolvent.

funding a trust — the process of reregistering ownership of assets into the name of a trust or causing a trust to become the designated beneficiary of insurance, retirement plans, or other assets permitting a beneficiary designation.

future interest — an interest that is not immediately owned and controlled by its recipient, such as when a trust is established for the recipient in lieu of an outright gift or bequest.

generation-skipping tax (GST) — a transfer tax imposed on a trust at the death of the trust beneficiary if the trust was created by anyone a generation or more older than the beneficiary and will pass to anyone a generation or more younger than the beneficiary. This tax is designed to prevent the tax-free passage of property from generation to generation.

gift tax — a transfer tax imposed upon the gift of property from one person to another. The gift tax is imposed in order to prevent the avoidance of estate taxes through lifetime transfers.

gift tax exclusion — an annual exclusion available for gifts of a present interest in property. The gift tax exclusion is $10,000 per donee as of 1999, but will increase with inflation.

gift-splitting — the ability of a married couple to treat a gift made by one of them as if it were made equally by each, so that each of their gift tax exclusions (or exemptions) can be utilized. Gift-splitting requires that each member of the couple file a gift tax return.

grantor — the creator of a trust; a settlor.

gross estate — the value of all assets in which the decedent had an interest at death.

guardian of the estate — a person appointed by the probate court to have control of property belonging to a minor or an incompetent adult.

guardian of the person — a person appointed by the probate court to have personal jurisdiction over a minor or incompetent adult.

health care surrogate form — in some states, a form that is the equivalent to a power of attorney for health care, wherein a specified person is delegated the responsibility for making health care decisions on behalf of the principal.

***in terrorem* clause** — a provision in an estate planning instrument that takes away a bequest from anyone who challenges the validity of the document. The provision only works when the amount forfeited is substantial enough to prevent the challenge or if the challenge is unsuccessful.

incident of ownership — a power or right with respect to an insurance policy that will cause the policy to be included in the insured's estate for death tax purposes.

Individual retirement account (IRA) — an account to which tax deductible contributions may be made and the earnings of which are not subject to current income tax, used to save for retirement. The funding and distributions from these accounts are subject to extremely detailed regulation by the Internal Revenue Code.

inheritance tax — a tax imposed at death upon the amount received by a beneficiary from a decedent.

inter vivos — Latin for "during life." A living trust is sometimes referred to as an *inter vivos* trust, though this expression is now somewhat archaic.

intestacy — dying without a valid will, causing the decedent's property to be distributed in accordance with the statutory law of intestate succession.

intestate succession, law of — the statutory provisions that govern how a person's probate estate is disposed of when he or she dies without a will.

irrevocable life insurance trust (ILIT) — an irrevocable trust that owns one or more life insurance policies, thus causing the policy proceeds to escape estate taxes upon the insured's death.

joint and mutual wills — typically, wills executed by a married couple that contain identical provisions and that restrict the right of the surviving spouse to change the manner in which the couple's assets are distributed. Not recommended for Illinois residents.

joint and survivor annuity — an annuity payable until the death of both annuitants, usually a married couple.

joint ownership — where two or more people own an undivided partial interest in property.

joint tenancy — in this book, a term embracing both joint tenancy with right of survivorship or tenancy by the entireties, which are the two types of ownership where the surviving owner or owners inherit the entire interest of the decedent by operation of law.

joint tenancy with right of survivorship — joint ownership where the interest of a deceased joint tenant passes to the surviving tenant or tenants.

land title trust — a manner of owning real property in a special kind of trust that is available in only a few states, including Illinois, where the concept originated. The primary benefits of this trust are privacy of ownership and facilitatation of financing secured by the real property.

last will and testament — a document that permits a person to dispose of property at death, appoint guardians for children, and designate an executor to administer the estate. A person's "last" will is the one most recently executed.

life tenant — the beneficiary of a trust entitled to receive income and, in some cases, principal distributions during his or her lifetime.

limited power of appointment — a power of appointment that does not permit the power holder to appoint property to the power holder or to the power holder's estate, creditors, or creditors of the estate. It is necessary to limit the power in this manner to keep the appointive property out of the power holder's estate for federal estate tax purposes.

living trust — a method of owning and disposing of property pursuant to a trust agreement so as to avoid both pre-death and post-death probate proceedings.

living will — a document by which a person expresses his or her desire not to be kept on life support in the event of a terminal illness.

lump-sum distribution — in a retirement plan context, the ability to receive all of a retirement plan account in a single payment.

make-up trust — a charitable remainder trust in which the amount passing outside of the family to charity at the end of the trust term is replaced by life insurance purchased using the savings created by the charitable deduction allowed at the inception of the trust.

marital property — in Illinois, generally, property earned as compensation during marriage. Marital property is treated differently than separate property in allocating a couple's assets upon a divorce.

medallion signature guarantee — most stockbrokers, banks, credit unions, and savings institutions participate in the medallion signature guarantee program, which allows a transfer agent to verify a person's signature in a security transaction. A medallion signature guarantee is required for almost all transfers of securities.

minor's exclusion trust — see Section 2503(c) trust.

permitted designated beneficiary — a term peculiar to this book, because the tax code term "designated beneficiary" is ambiguous. See designated beneficiary.

per stirpes — Latin for "by the roots." A distribution to person's descendants *per stirpes* is divided equally among the person's children, but if one of the children predeceases that person, the share that would otherwise have passed to the child instead passes equally among the deceased child's children. The same rule applies if any descendant otherwise entitled to take is not then living. If a deceased descendant has no descendants, the share passes equally to that descendant's siblings.

pick-up tax — a death tax imposed by a state that is equal to the credit allowed by the federal estate tax system for state death taxes. A state (such as Illinois) whose death tax is equal to the state death tax credit, and that imposes no other death taxes, is said to be a "pick-up tax state."

plan participant — the person who creates an IRA or who has an interest in a qualified retirement plan account.

pooled income fund — an investment fund created by a charitable organization that provides the investor an annual payment, typically for life, with the remaining funds passing to the charity, resulting in a charitable income tax deduction at the time the original investment is made.

post-mortem — Latin for "after death."

pourover will — a will whose primary purpose is to cause the transfer of any probate assets at death to a trust created by the testator.

power of appointment — a right given to a trust beneficiary to designate how the trust property will eventually be distributed. A testamentary power of appointment is exercised in the beneficiary's will and provides for the distribution of the trust property after the beneficiary's death. Some powers of appointment can be exercised during lifetime and provide for the distribution of the trust property during the beneficiary's life or after his or her death.

power of attorney — a legal instrument by which a person appoints an agent (or attorney-in-fact) to act on that person's behalf. Typically powers of attorney deal with property or health care.

power of attorney for health care — an instrument by which a person appoints an agent to make health care decisions in the event the person is incapable of making those decisions personally.

power of attorney for property — an instrument by which a person appoints an agent to make decisions concerning financial matters in the event the person is incapable of making those decisions personally.

present interest — any interest in gifted property allowing the recipient to immediately own, control, and enjoy the entire gift. Gifts of a present interest qualify for the annual gift tax exclusion.

principal — in estate planning this word has two distinct meanings. In the context of a power of attorney, the principal is the person who creates the power, naming an agent. Principal also refers to the property held in a trust or other account, as distinguished from the income that principal earns.

probate — the process by which the solely-owned assets of a decedent (or incompetent person) are administered. Also refers to the court with jurisdiction over those types of proceedings.

probate avoidance — a manner of owning property so that it will not be subject to a probate proceeding upon death or incompetency. Probate avoidance devices include joint tenancy with right of survivorship, tenancy by the entireties, trusts, and property that passes pursuant to a beneficiary designation, such as life insurance, retirement plans, or IRAs.

probate property — property held in sole ownership or tenancy in common, or property such as insurance and retirement accounts that is payable to the decedent's executor or estate.

qualified domestic trust (QDOT) — a form of trust needed when the surviving spouse is a non-citizen in order to qualify the property passing to that spouse for the estate tax marital deduction.

qualified retirement plan — a retirement plan that meets certain IRS rules and regulations so that contributions to it are tax free and no current income tax is payable on its earnings. Examples include profit-sharing, Keogh, 401(k), 403(b), and pension plans.

qualified terminable interest property trust (QTIP) — a special form of marital trust that permits the first spouse to die to determine the ultimate beneficiaries of the trust following the death of the surviving spouse.

recalculation method — a method of computing the required minimum distribution from a retirement plan that allows the participant's life expectancy to be recomputed each year.

remainder interest — the interest in a trust that passes upon the termination of the previous beneficiary's interest. Typically, after the first beneficiary has enjoyed an interest in the trust for life, the property remaining in the trust at the beneficiary's death constitutes the remainder interest.

remaindermen — The beneficiaries entitled to receive the remainder interest in a trust. The identity of the remaindermen can usually not be determined with certainty until the death of the life beneficiary.

required beginning date — the date on which a participant in a retirement plan is required to begin making withdrawals from the plan. In most cases, this date is April 1 of the year following the year in which the plan participant attains age 70½.

required minimum distribution — the amount a participant in a retirement plan is required to withdraw per year once the required beginning date is reached.

Roth IRA — introduced by the Taxpayer Relief Act of 1997, a form of retirement plan where contributions to the plan are not deductible, but the plan earnings and distributions are not taxable.

second-to-die life insurance — insurance that pays a death benefit upon the death of the second to die of two individuals, usually spouses.

Section 2503(c) trust — also known as a minor's exclusion trust, or minor's trust, a special type of trust designed to qualify any transfers to it for the $10,000 annual gift tax exclusion.

self-declaration of trust — a trust where the creator of the trust is also its trustee.

separate property — for purposes of Illinois law relating to divorce, property that was owned by the spouse prior to the marriage, property received by gift or inheritance during the marriage, and any earnings and appreciation on all such property.

settlor — the creator of a trust; a grantor.

signature guarantee — see medallion signature guarantee.

single-fund trust — a trust held for the benefit of two or more beneficiaries that will eventually be divided among those beneficiaries. Used primarily to care for a person's children financially until all have achieved financial independence.

small estate affidavit — a form that can be used to collect probate assets in small estates (in Illinois, under $50,000) and avoid a formal probate proceeding.

sole ownership — ownership of property in a person's own name.

specific bequest — a gift at death of a specific amount of money or a specifically identified property item.

spendthrift clause — a trust provision insulating the trust's assets from the claims of the beneficiary's creditors. A trust containing such a provision is often called a spendthrift trust.

spousal rollover — the rollover by the plan participant's spouse of the lump sum proceeds of a qualified retirement plan or IRA to his or her own IRA, which allows the deferral of the income tax that would otherwise be payable.

statutory power of attorney — form of power of attorney created by state legislation, designed to provide uniformity and ready acceptance by financial and health care institutions.

statutory share — also called a forced share, the right given to a surviving spouse by statute to receive a percentage of the deceased spouse's estate despite receiving a smaller bequest (or no bequest) in the decedent's will. In Illinois, the share is one third if there are children, one half if there are not.

stepped-up basis — used to describe the (usually) increased cost basis of an asset upon its owner's death, when the federal estate tax value of the asset becomes the cost basis for determining gain or loss upon disposition.

stock power — an instrument used to transfer ownership of a stock certificate, more formally known as an assignment separate from certificate.

substituted judgment laws — state legislation that grants to guardians for an incompetent person the power to create estate planning instruments for that person, such as wills and trusts.

supplemental needs trust — a special type of trust that provides for the special, non-support needs of a person also receiving government assistance, designed to withstand efforts by the governmental agency to obtain reimbursement.

survivor (or survivorship) life insurance — see second-to-die insurance.

tangible personal property — personal and household effects such as clothing, jewelry, china, silver, crystal, art work, electronic devices, furniture, furnishings, etc. Does not include stocks, bonds, cash, and similar property, which are called intangible personal property.

tax avoidance — the ordering of a person's affairs so as to minimize or eliminate taxes. Tax avoidance is legal; tax evasion is not.

taxable estate — the value of all of a person's property subject to an estate tax, less permitted deductions.

tenancy by the entireties — a form of ownership similar to joint tenancy, but which protects the property from the creditors of either tenant, although not from claims on which both tenants are liable.

tenancy in common — a form of ownership where each tenant separately owns an equal undivided interest in property that does not automatically pass at death to the remaining tenant or tenants.

Totten trust — a form of ownership in which a beneficiary is designated to receive the property upon death; similar to a payable on death (POD) account.

transfer tax — a term encompassing a wide variety of taxes designed to tax the transfer of property from one person to another. Transfer taxes include estate, inheritance, gift, and generation-skipping taxes.

trust — an arrangement by which property is owned by a trustee for the benefit of the trust beneficiaries pursuant to the provisions of a trust agreement.

trustee — the person, bank, or trust company empowered to hold, invest, and distribute trust property.

unified transfer tax — the method by which the federal government taxes property transfers, in which the estate tax and gift tax operate as part of a single tax structure.

Uniform Transfers to Minors Act (UTMA) — a method of transferring property to minors that does not require a trust. Commonly referred to as a custodian account. Similar to the Uniform Gifts to Minors Act formerly used in Illinois.

wealth replacement trust — see make-up trust.

will — a document that permits a person to dispose of property at death, appoint guardians for children, and designate an executor to administer the estate.

Index

(Page numbers in italics refer to glossary entries)

guardian (*continued*)
  appointment in power of attorney for
    property, 35
  appointment in will, for minors, 30
  of the estate, 99, *163*
  of the person, 99, *163*
  powers of, 16
  selection of, 101–102

guardianship, 15–16
  avoidance of, 22

health care power of attorney. *See*
    power of attorney for health care

health care surrogate form, 36, *163*

incidents of ownership, 114–115, *163*

income payments
  from charitable split-interest trust,
    142
  from child's trust, 80, 81
  from estate tax shelter trust, 60,
    70–71, *form language* 73, 74
  from generation-skipping trust, 87,
    88
  from marital trust, 45, 75, 77
  from §2503(c) trust, 108, 110–111,
    112
  from trust for descendants, 78,
    104–105

income tax. *See* federal income tax

individual retirement account (IRA),
    163. See also retirement plan

Illinois estate tax, 41–42

inheritance tax, 41, *164*

insurance. *See* life insurance

in terrorem clause, 96–97, *163*

intestacy, 13–15, *164*

intestate succession, 6, 13–14, 95, *164*

IRA, *163. See also* retirement plan

irrevocable life insurance trust (ILIT),
    116–117, 119–123, 143, *164*
  avoidance of estate tax by, 116–117,
    119–121
  diagram, 120
  disadvantages of, 123
  gift tax and, 121–122
  similarity to estate tax shelter trust,
    119–120

joint and mutual will, 77, *164*

joint and survivor annuity, 125, *164*

joint ownership, 6–8, *164*

joint tenancy, 6–8, *164*
  disadvantages of, 62–63
  estate taxability of, 42–43, 59
  simultaneous death, 8–9

joint tenancy with right of survivorship,
    6–7, 8, *164*

Keogh plan. *See* retirement plan

land title trust, 27–28, *164*

last will and testament, *164. See also*
    will

life expectancy tables, 128, 130

life insurance, 113–118
  accidental death insurance, 118, *159*
  beneficiary designation, 9, 23–24, 65,
    114–115
  compared to retirement plan, 113–114
  creditor protection of, 115, 148
  estate taxability of, 43, 114,
    115–116, 117
  incidents of ownership, 114–115, *163*
  as investment vehicle, 113–114

transfer tax, 41, *170*

transfer tax avoidance
  by charitable gifts, 141–144
  by disclaimer, 60–61
  by estate tax shelter trust, 53–59
  by generation-skipping trust, 82, 86,
    89–90
  by gifts, 103–107
  by irrevocable life insurance trust,
    116–117, 119–121
  by §2503(c) trust, 108–112

transfer tax system, 41–52

trust, 17–18, *170*
  as non-probate property, 9
  charitable trusts, 141–144
  for child, 80–82
  creditor protection of, 20, 75, 81, 85, 88,
    100, 145
  for descendants, 78–80, 104–105, *168*
  estate taxability of, 44
  estate tax shelter trust. *See* estate tax shel-
    ter trust
  funding. *See* funding of trust
  generation-skipping. *See* generation-skip-
    ping trusts
  for grandchildren, 84–85
  income tax rates of, 111
  irrevocable life insurance trust. *See* irre-
    vocable life insurance trust
  land title trust, 27–28, *164*
  for life, 81–82. *See also* generation-skip-
    ping trusts
  living. *See* living trust
  marital deduction trust. *See* marital trust
  Medicaid qualifying trust, 153
  for minors. *See* Section 2503(c) trust
  misconceptions about, 21
  offshore trust, 147–148
  qualified domestic trust, 45, *167*
  qualified terminable interest trust, 76, *167*
  remaindermen, 72, 91, *167*
  §2503(c) trust. *See* Section 2503(c) trust
  self-declaration of, 18

supplemental needs trust, *169*
Totten, 9, *170*

trustee, *170*
  appointment of, 99–100
  corporate, 21, 34, 100, 101
  duties of, 98

unified transfer tax, 48, *170*

Uniform Transfers to Minors Act, 85, 112,
    170

wealth replacement trust. *See* make-up trust

will, 6, 30–31, 94, *170*
  absence of, 13–14
  appointment of executor in, 98
  appointment of guardians in, 99
  compared to trust, 18, 19, 20, 21, 22, 94
  filing of, 19, 30
  joint and mutual, 77, *164*
  joint tenancy assets not controlled by, 62
  living. *See* living will
  pourover, 18–19, 30–31
  as primary dispositive document, 30–31

will contest, 10

withdrawal
  from child's trust, 80
  from descendant's trust, 104
  from generation-skipping trust, 91
  from grandchild's trust, 85
  from irrevocable life insurance trust, 122
  from marital trust, 76
  from retirement plan, 126–132
  from §2503(c) trust, 109
  withholding of, 85

Laurence J. Kline graduated from the University of Michigan
Law School in 1971 after completing his undergraduate education
at Northwestern University. Since then he has concentrated his legal
career in the areas of estate planning and estate and trust administration, first at one of Chicago's leading trust departments, then at two
large firms, and most recently as a founding partner of the firm of
Carroll, Kline & Wall, an estate planning and administration
"boutique" firm serving the Chicago area.

The author is a member of the Illinois Bar and the Chicago
Estate Planning Council, and has served as chairman of the Trust
Law Committee of the Chicago Bar Association. He and his wife
Cindy reside in Indian Head Park, Illinois.

Order Form

Additional copies of *Disinheriting Uncle Sam* are available at $14.95 per copy. Quantity discounts are available for three copies or more. Inquire by telephone at 312-214-9002 or by letter to: **Vireo Publishing, 70 W. Madison Street, Suite 620, Chicago, Illinois 60602.**

Name and Address

_____

_____

_____

Telephone number (optional)

( )_____

Illinois Residents

☐ Please send me one copy. Enclosed is my check in the amount of $19.15, which includes 8% sales tax of $1.20 and $3.00 shipping & handling.

☐ Please send me two copies. Enclosed is my check in the amount of $35.30, which includes 8% sales tax of $2.40 and $3.00 shipping & handling.

Non-Illinois Residents

☐ Please send me one copy. Enclosed is my check in the amount of $17.95, which includes $3.00 shipping & handling.

☐ Please send me two copies. Enclosed is my check in the amount of $32.90, which includes $3.00 shipping & handling.

(Cut here or photocopy)